TURNBULL SCHOOL, SAN MATEO, CALIFORNIA, RICHARD SPERISEN, ART SUPERVISOR

Mr. C. Lloyd Bailey, Executive Director, United States Committee for UNICEF, Mr. Philip J. Vandor, Principal of Turnbull School, San Mateo, California, and children admire a "mural in the round" which the children created with 5,000 handmade ceramic tiles.

MURALS
for SCHOOLS

SHARING CREATIVE EXPERIENCES

ARNE W. RANDALL

Professor of Art
California State College
Hayward, California

Illustrated by the Author

DAVIS PUBLICATIONS, INC., WORCESTER, MASSACHUSETTS, U.S.A.

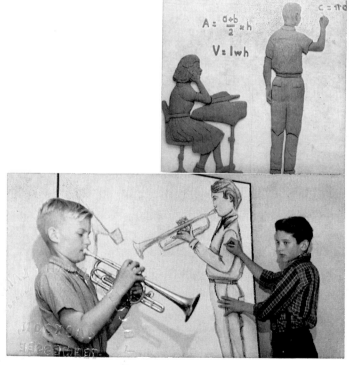

DEDICATION

To my loving wife, Florence,
and our children—
Marlene, Reino, Carole, and Jane.

Acknowledgments

I especially wish to acknowledge the innumerable friends who have expressed a need for this book and those who have so generously made suggestions, provided photographs, read copy, lent encouragement and assurance whenever it was needed. I wish to recognize my former colleagues of the Office of Education, Department of Health, Education, and Welfare, Washington, D.C., and particularly Dr. Effie Bathhurst who has been a constant source of inspiration and assistance. I am also indebted to Dr. Karl Schlicher, Head, Department of Art, Stephen F. Austin State College, Nacogdoches, Texas; to Richard Sperisen, Art Supervisor, San Mateo Public School System, San Mateo, California, and to Reino Randall, Department of Art, Central Washington College, Ellensburg, Washington. My present and former students are to be commended for their willingness to experiment with murals in class and as teachers in their own classrooms. And, I particularly wish to thank my wife, Florence, without whose assistance this book would never have been written.

A.W.R.

Introduction

It is hoped that this book will serve as an introduction to mural projects for schools and in some small way kindle the creative spark in this popular school activity. No attempt has been made to give all of the information for a completed mural activity as each teacher and each group of children will want to express, in their own way, with their own materials, the ideas they have. It is also the feeling of the author that there is no one way to provide creative activities since no two school situations are the same. Other values might be derived from a mural activity that may be of greater importance to the youngsters than the mere production of a pictorial mural. The individual as well as the group needs and developments that are encountered during the activity can, in many instances, be very far-reaching. It is with this thought in mind that this book has been assembled using photographs, illustrations, and text to serve only as suggestions. The direction taken on any mural activity should come from the teacher's planning with children. The creative spirit of children needs only to be released.

A.W.R.

Table of Contents

UNIVERSITY OF WASHINGTON PRESS, SEATTLE, WASHINGTON, FROM "CREATING WITH PAPER" BY PAULINE JOHNSON

EAST BOLTON SCHOOL, COWLEY COUNTY, KANSAS. WILDA L. PATTERSON, TEACHER

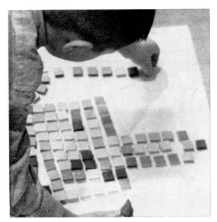

1

The Mural

Murals are fun to make! There may be a number of reasons for providing a mural activity. A mural may be made purely for the pleasure children derive from creating. Perhaps they wish to decorate spaces that are dull and uninteresting in the hall or classroom. A mural may be used to motivate interest in other subject areas. A mural activity may be provided to bring together into one large illustration the ideas of many individuals. It may also help children to learn to work together. Children may need to learn to work freely with large areas and a variety of materials. A mural may be the culminating activity that helps children to review a vital experience or relive an impression of a trip the class has taken.

A mural makes an effective wall decoration. Usually it is a large piece of work painted directly on the wall or applied to other flat material which is fastened to the wall. This may be done by the use of one or a great variety of media.

Murals differ from other painted pictures in several respects. Some murals are designed to decorate a particular wall surface. They should be considered in relation to the surface they are to decorate and become an integral part of it. A painting or photograph, on the other hand, is separate from the wall on which it hangs and usually independent of its surrounding areas.

Murals may be started in kindergarten. In each succeeding grade the techniques become more challenging. School murals usually consist of two types: the border mural and the panel mural. The effectiveness of either type depends to a large degree on the space, color, texture, design and techniques employed.

1

BORDER MURALS

A border mural may be a long continuous unit with a relatively complete story. Usually it conveys a central thought throughout, with the sequence often running from left to right. When several important points are highlighted in the mural, the interest is spread over the entire surface. Occasionally one idea in the mural may be more prominent than several areas of lesser importance, and the interest therefore is directed toward this particular spot. The story of the westward movement in United States history could be shown on a continuous border. The spot to be highlighted would depend on what the children decided should have most emphasis; that is, what to them seemed important or interesting.

The tack board above the chalkboard or bulletin board can be used as semipermanent mural space since children cannot readily reach this high area. Also, wall space that would otherwise remain unused can be transferred into a mural area such as the space between windows.

The relationship of space, color, line, and texture helps emphasize continuity in the continuous border mural. The mural's continuity may be also held together by a common background, uniform-sized objects or figures, or repetition of certain colors.

Possible subjects for continuous murals:

Stories:

The Seven Dwarfs	Uncle Remus
Little Red Riding Hood	Pinocchio
Peter Pan	Hiawatha
Cinderella	The Night Before Christmas
Bambi	Three Bears
Peter and the Wolf	Nursery Rhymes

Themes:

Holidays	Conservation
Recreation	Utilities
Occupations	Farm
Safety	Foods
Communication	Health
Seasons	Transportation
Industries	Community Helpers

The composite border mural consists of a series of separate pictures on a central theme with little or no direct sequence of ideas. Each child makes a picture or portion of the story. Papers for the scenes are divided into the desired size. Each student takes his paper to a working place and works on his portion of the composition. The finished pieces are fastened together by paste, by masking tape, or by other means to complete the mural. Continuous lines or objects forming the background may be drawn on the completed mural to tie it together.

Some groups may wish to maintain uniform size of figures and objects on the separate pictures. By using a common background and common colors the same theme may be carried throughout the mural. The standards agreed to by the youngsters will naturally vary with the interest and experience of the group.

Possible subjects for composite murals:

These are sometimes known as the crazy quilt or patchwork designs, usually with no top nor bottom. Figures and objects may be placed on mural in any position.

Jungle Animals	Plant Forms
Flowers	Animals
Fish or Sea Life	Abstract Designs
Birds	Leaves
Vegetables	City Life

PANEL MURALS

A panel mural may consist of one picture or a series of related pictures. One large panel might cover an area from ceiling to the floor. Another may reach from wall to wall. The vacant spaces between windows and doors, or in corners of the room, may be filled with tall narrow panels. A long narrow panel might be covered with a series of small murals placed vertically or horizontally. Square murals may sometimes be placed vertically in series, at intervals, according to the available space.

Each picture in a series might depict a different phase of the main subject. The collective theme might be transportation with individual pictures portraying airplanes, ships, automobiles, trucks, or trains from the very first to the latest designs. The only thing these pictures might have in common would be the size of paper and the fact that they were arranged in series. Stories, themes, or patchwork and crazy quilt ideas, make excellent panel murals.

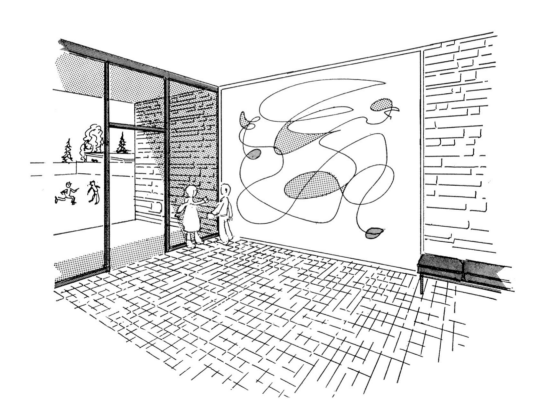

The beauty of a classroom may be enhanced if mural space around the windows is provided. These panels may be such that they can be removed for painting.

Panels that have permanent mounts simplify renewing and replacing murals.

5

FITTING MURALS TO SPACE

The size and placement of the mural should conform to the principles of good design. Children should help decide this point as soon as they are interested. In the primary grades, however, children are usually not concerned with size and location of a mural. Their interest lies principally in creating. The teacher is more responsible for the size and placement. Students in upper grades will become more aware of the effect produced by proper size and placement of a mural. In selecting a place for a mural try, if possible, to choose a place which will assure the desired attention for the finished work. It should face the light. The chosen space should be measured to determine how large to make the mural. For instance, if a very large mural is placed on a small wall the eye cannot always perceive the total picture or story it is to tell. Consequently, the purpose of the mural is often defeated or diluted. Oversize figures and objects on a mural in a small room will have a tendency to depress and dwarf the room.

The arrangement of the room should be considered. It makes a difference whether the mural is to fill a bare wall or balance another decoration. A mural should be so planned that it will comply with the basic fundamentals of wall decoration and automatically become a part of the wall. The shapes and positions of the figures and objects in the mural will usually be governed by the shape of the space where the mural will be placed. A center of interest is often planned according to the size, placement, and color of the mural so the eye will easily move from one object to the next.

The large expanse of the mural and use of media in a bold way encourage the space to be filled, eliminating useless details. If the main objects are too small there will be too much open space occupied with uninteresting background. While discussing the mural with the children, it can be pointed out that the background should become a part of the composition. Too much space around the figures tends to dwarf them, while, on the other hand, if they are crowded the beauty of the background may be lost.

Various kinds of bulletin boards and chalkboards, a popular word for blackboard, make excellent areas for murals. They may vary according to the size of the available space. A variety of such areas in a classroom enables many children to have their work exhibited.

Chalkboards

A chalkboard is an appropriate place for a mural. If there is chalkboard space that can be spared for a time, a mural can be drawn directly on it. It provides the firmest and smoothest backing for painting. In order to avoid damaging a chalkboard, it may be advisable to consult the principal before using any liquids. The preliminary sketch may be drawn in chalk and the colors filled in with a mixture of powdered poster paint. This makes durable murals, yet may be easily washed off. Murals also may be drawn on paper and taped over the chalkboard.

Bulletin Boards

There are many kinds of bulletin boards; some are permanent, others are movable. The mural can be done on paper either before or after it is placed on the board. If at all possible the paper on which the mural is being made should be left intact until the work is completed, since some papers tear easily and lose their crispness when handled too much. The bulletin board is an excellent place for cut-paper murals, as the cutouts can be pinned in place, changed, and removed when necessary.

Most classrooms have bulletin boards. Should a class want to make its own a variety of materials is readily obtainable including: celotex, masonite, plywood, pine panels, pegboard, corrugated paper, easel, pipe display rack, slat, panel, or sectional screens. To make bulletin board displays attractive, colorful and textured materials can often be secured at little or no cost in the school supply room or local stores. Among such materials are textured cloths, different kinds of papers, colored yarn, corrugated cardboard, rope, string, burlap, metallic thread, or wire. Equipment that might be needed for making bulletin boards includes staplers, rubber cement, straight pins, scissors, paints, paintbrushes, rulers, pens, and ink.

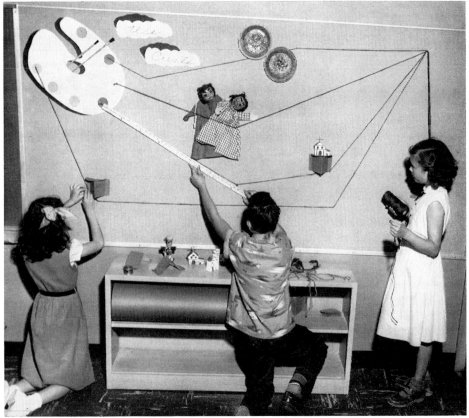

COURTESY ALAMEDA COUNTY SCHOOLS, HAYWARD, CALIFORNIA

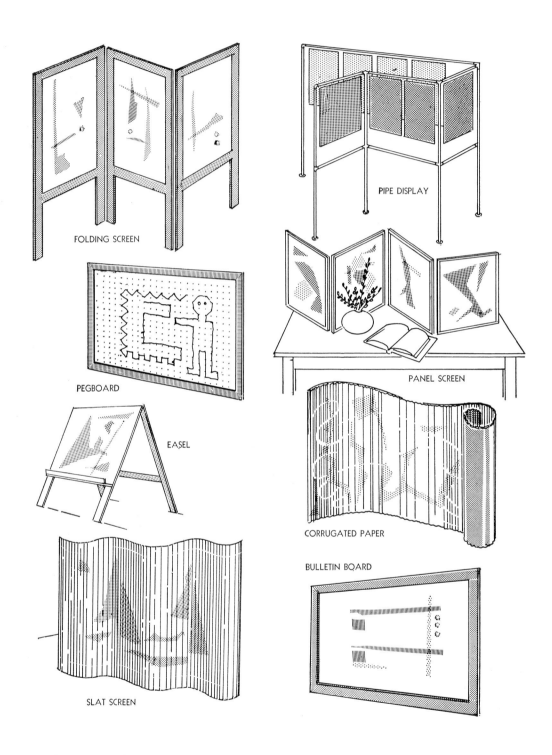

FOLDING SCREEN

PIPE DISPLAY

PEGBOARD

PANEL SCREEN

EASEL

CORRUGATED PAPER

SLAT SCREEN

BULLETIN BOARD

8

This simple flannel board was made with outing flannel stretched and pasted over cardboard. Assorted fabrics cut into different shapes and sizes were always available on the table for the students to experiment with design.

Flannel Boards

A flannel or felt board is a lot of fun. One may be purchased from school supply houses. They may be made in workshop classes or by teachers. Inexpensive cotton, nylon or outing flannel, felt, or a wool material may be stretched over a surface of wallboard, cardboard, plywood, building board, or old window screen. The material should be pasted to the surface or tacked at the edges to keep it relatively tight.

Since the fuzzy surface of flannel will hold pieces of fabric and other textured materials, figures and geometric shapes may be cut and arranged on the flannel board in a creative way. Objects that have a smooth surface such as shapes cut from paper can be used if a piece of sandpaper is pasted to the back of the cutout figure. The sandpaper will stick to the flannel.

Stage Backdrops

A backdrop for a stage may be made of firm building wallboard or canvas stretched over a large frame. Such a mural can be replaced each year, giving other children an opportunity to plan, to develop, and to complete future backdrops for the stage. It may include movable panels used for changes of scenes. In a school in the State of Washington, children decided to have an operetta. They wrote their songs, composed the music, and painted large mural panels that were used as backdrops for their stage production.

DESIGN

The basic elements of design may become an important facet in murals made by older children. However, the pursuit of design should not hold precedence over the satisfaction children derive from working on the mural. In order to achieve quality of design, children can be taught relatively early to study the design and color found in other graphic arts. In addition, the school can provide a wide variety of famous pictures of old masters as well as contemporary artists. These may be discussed in the class for color, for design, and for composition rather than to learn the time when the picture was painted and the life of the artist. Many teachers have begun to use such methods as "picture of the week" to broaden the children's knowledge of good art. Even very young children will enjoy picture study. It must be remembered that all children respond in their own way to color and to design. Teachers should encourage each child to express his own individuality rather than to copy compositional characteristics of other paintings.

SELECTING COLORS FOR MURALS

Depending on the age level, some of the suggestions discussed on color may be helpful purely for the learning process involved. Children should be encouraged to express themselves freely with whatever colors they enjoy using. As they mature there are some factors pertaining to color which students may wish to consider in making their murals. Older children appreciate the importance and emphasis of color distribution. They should have the opportunity of choosing their own colors. Color lends itself to discussion. If there is no preliminary discussion all children may choose the same colors. This can be the beginning of color study.

Children's keen interest in color may be a source of pleasure in producing effective murals. After making several murals, children begin to realize the important part that color plays. They discover, for example, that their murals will be more interesting if the color areas are not too broken. They learn the value of having some dark, some light hues; some bright, some dull shades to produce the effects they desire.

Children can discover that any color is good if used in proper relationships, even though it may be uninteresting or monotonous if used alone. They may want to repeat colors across the mural. If too much of one color appears at one end and not enough on the other, the picture may look unbalanced. Complimentary color combinations can be carried throughout the mural in a pleasing arrangement without strong color oppositions. Light colors may sometimes be painted on dark or different shades for contrast, or vice versa. The quality of the color depends almost entirely upon the relationship of other colors placed beside it. Here are some of the ways in which colors may be used. In addition to these, children will discover other related facts about color if they are encouraged to work freely with it.

Colors may be blended with other colors.

A color may be grayed by adding its complement.

A feeling of warmth may be added by using colors related to yellow.

A feeling of coolness may be added by using colors related to blue.

Colors may be contrasted with various shades and values of the same color.

Plaids may be made of various colors.

A color may be supported by placing it near one or more related colors.

A color may be accented by placing it with one or more neutral colors, such as black, white, or gray.

Colors may be repeated to achieve unity.

Many shades may be made of one color by adding black.

Many tints may be made of one color by adding white.

The teacher may want to help children realize that colors for a mural should be related as much as possible to the colors in the room and the type of room in which it is to be placed. Murals probably more than any other graphic activity in a classroom can stimulate the study of color and its various effects on the cheerfulness of the room, the attitudes toward study, and the physical condition of the boys and girls. The teacher may wish to take advantage of such learning situations.

"Children at Play," a laminated plastic mural panel in the auditorium of the Bronx Public School No. 8, New York City. Executed by Stuyvesant Van Veen, New York City.

Schoolrooms on the north side of the building may need bright warm colors. Murals for a study hall or library should have soft quiet colors. Brightly-colored murals may not be conducive to the quietness and concentration which are essential in a library or study hall. When children share in making these rooms more attractive, they are more at home in them and have the feeling of serving a worthwhile purpose. The school librarian without art training can utilize the art department in helping to make it an attractive room.

Active, brightly-colored murals spaced to break the monotony of long dark gloomy corridors will create a cheerful attitude and have a stimulating effect on pupils. The atmosphere of a cafeteria may be made pleasing through design and color in a mural.

Pupils may find it educationally worthwhile to discuss color usage with their local paint dealers who often have charts and literature describing the rooms for which colors are suggested. Pupils may also find practical color information in their school art books and encyclopedias.

Texture instead of color on a college campus plan aids blind students and visitors to orient themselves to the buildings and walks on the campus.

BACKGROUND MATERIALS FOR MURALS

Material on which a mural is made is important. Insofar as possible, materials found in the classroom should be used. Sometimes it is necessary to purchase the proper paper. Building paper, newsprint, and wallpaper are usually the best and cheapest papers available. All of these may be found in the school community. Other backing papers include: colored construction paper, butcher paper, corrugated cardboard, drawing paper, poster board, oatmeal paper. Visit an art supply or school supply store for other suggestions regarding papers that may be available.

Heavy wrapping paper and building paper are firm papers to which water-soluble paints or calcimine will adhere and usually will not wrinkle when wet. Almost any paper is good for chalk. Shiny or slick-surfaced paper is less suitable for painting or coloring.

The back of wallpaper is used by some teachers for crayon, for chalk, or for cut-paper murals. Since wallpaper tears easily it is advisable to have it wider and longer then the drawing so it may be trimmed. A good way to handle wallpaper is to measure convenient heights for the children to work and to tape the paper to the chalkboard or bulletin board. If the floor is smooth and clean children enjoy working on it.

Corrugated cardboard makes interesting background for murals. Colorful and unusual designs may be painted on this type of cardboard with tempera paint, showcard paint, poster paint, or water colors.

A wallpaper catalog provides the texture for this mural made on a wrapping-paper background.

13

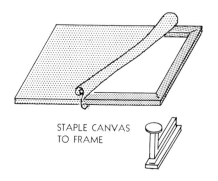

STAPLE CANVAS
TO FRAME

TACK CANVAS TO PLYWOOD

PASTE CANVAS
TO BUILDING BOARD

Various types of cloth may be used for a mural. Factory cotton, sign cloth, sack-cloth, or old sheets pasted to cardboard are suitable. Designs may be sewn on cloth with bright bits of wool, felt, or yarn. This type of background should not be too large since it requires much handling. It is also helpful to place it in a frame to keep it flat. When painting on a cloth background the material should be tacked or fastened securely to a wall or table. Before painting, the cloth should be covered with a thin coat of diluted glue or sizing. This preliminary coating is used to stiffen the cloth and reduce the porous quality. The preliminary drawing may be sketched on the cloth with pencil, charcoal, tempera, poster paint, or calcimine.

Heavy unbleached muslin sheeting is ideal for paintings. The material may be stretched on the floor and sketches made with charcoal. The large areas may be painted with an inexpensive, heavy casein paint.

Canvas is a practical material for murals. Burlap sacking is another strong, coarse weave material that is easy for children to handle. Burlap lends itself to painting, to yarn decorations, and to felt appliqués.

Other background materials that may be used are: pressed board of various types, window shades, or old signs.

Many teachers have discovered new and unusual materials for backgrounds by surveying the community to see what is available. Such materials can then be adapted as the background for the mural project.

PERMANENT MURALS

Wall space can sometimes be filled with a permanent mural. The mural should be adapted to the room or to the space it is to cover and complement the architectural harmony of the room. Permanent murals may be painted directly on plaster, on wallboard, on wood panel, or on either paper or cloth, glued directly to the wall. It is helpful to plan every detail before its final execution. A small-scale plan of the mural composition may be made to establish proportions to the wall space.

There are two techniques used professionally which can be used to paint the mural directly on the wall: painting on the wet mortar or painting on a dry plaster. While painting on wet mortar is the most durable type, under most circumstances its application is too complicated for use in elementary and secondary school classrooms.

Wet fresco in its pure form is painting on damp, fresh, lime plaster. The lime of the plaster provides a binder for the drying of the fresco and forms a calcium carbonate which combines the pigment with the material of the wall. The muralist makes sketches of each subject he plans to include in the final mural. These he works out to scale. This preliminary detail work is called "cartoon." Hence, the current use of the word cartoon means a hasty sketch of a subject which is associated with the comic sketch of today. Cartoons of the same dimensions as the fresco are transferred to the rough plastered wall. On this, the finished coat of plaster made of fine sand, lime, and

A blind child reads the Braille inscription over the "Touch-and-Go" mural created by Edgar Britton which is set into the wall of the entrance to the infirmary at the Colorado School for the Deaf and Blind in Colorado Springs, Colorado. The texture and relief found in this series of brass repousse panels of flora and fauna with a background of blue and green Italian glass mosaic offers pleasing tactile experiences for blind children.

15

Wall pictures played an important part in the cave dweller's society. These primitive people lived, not in houses as we do today, but in caves, many of which have been found in France, Austria, Spain, and other countries. On the walls of these cave homes, paintings still exist which show that art was a highly functional, natural, and integral part of their lives.

In America one of the primitive arts of the past is the pictograph or picture writing of the native Southwest Indians. In addition to voice and gesture, primitive man had a need for communicating his ideas through a form of writing. Picture writing was one of the earliest forms of transmitting ideas. It was used by Indians as well as other civilizations such as the Sumerians, settlers of Mesopotamia as early as 3200 B.C.

Pictographs were carved on stone walls with primitive tools under great handicaps. This early art expression may be considered the beginning of mural art.

16

The above portion of the mural series in The Museum of Texas Technological College, depicts the early period of the South Plains, Lubbock, Texas. Peter Hurd, well-known muralist, did the work in wet fresco, using the same materials and methods employed in the Sistine Chapel in Italy.

Prior to 1890, except for the religious paintings of John LaFarge, very little mural painting was done in United States. Following LaFarge, such painters as Kenyon Cox, T. H. Benton, Boardman Robinson, Arthur B. Davies, N. C. Wyeth, and Flashfield became popular. Mexican fresco painters Rivera and Orozco aroused new interest in the art in the 1920's.

In the United States the modern mural became popular in the 1930's when the government established a permanent Section of Painting and Sculpture for the decoration of public buildings. This policy not only stimulated mural painting but attracted some of the best artists in the country, among them George Biddle, John Steuart Curry, H. V. Poor, Paul Sample, Maurice Sterne, and Peter Hurd. Murals are now extensively employed in decorating federal buildings. Private business is using murals in offices, lobbies, and factories.

marble dust is applied in small sections. The colors become part of the wall when combined with the wet plaster. Mural painters must draw accurately, quickly, and know exactly what they are going to do before beginning since plaster sets quickly. Only the space which is to be painted in a day is plastered, as it must be smooth and freshly done.

Painting on dry plaster may be easier than painting on the wet mortar. If the mural is to be done in oil, Ralph Mayer states in "The Artist's Handbook of Materials and Techniques:"

> Modern authorities on paint technology seem to favor a thin priming coat of specially designed paint applied directly to the plaster instead of a sizing . . . ready-mixed primers, second coats, and finish coats bearing the labels of well-established reliable makers are most likely to be well-balanced materials made in accordance with the most approved standards. . . . Requirements for a plaster primer include permanent binding or attachment to plaster, production of a uniform surface upon which subsequent painting will take well, good covering power, and not too great penetration into the wall surface.[1]

Another teacher reports that one or two coats of flat, oil paint will serve as sizing prior to the actual painting.

There are innumerable practices for applying tempera paint directly to a plastered wall, each of which should be studied with care since there are apt to be chemical reactions between the various pigments, the sizing, and the wall surface. One of the following may be able to tell you where to secure such information: local paint store, plasterers' union, art supply dealers, or manufacturers of paint. Some teachers have reported that the following proportions have proved relatively successful. The plaster is first painted with a sizing. To make the tempera adhere to the wall two parts water to one egg yolk is a desirable binding medium (this mixture of water and egg yolk is stirred into the tempera). A mixture of glue (or casein) and water in the proportion of one to ten may also be used. The best procedure is to make a thick paste by mixing the paint pigment with water, then add the egg yolk immediately before painting. Mix only the amount of paint anticipated to be used at the one painting.

Other basic pigments, such as wax crayon, chalk, and tempera, may be made permanent by melting wax and allowing it to penetrate into the wall. Dry tempera and chalk may be mixed with clear lacquer, varnish, or shellac. Water-base, latex-base wall paints or oil-base paints may also be used for semipermanent or permanent murals.

Mosaic is a type of art done by arranging many-shaped and multicolored pieces, such as stone, glass, marble, tile, wood, or other materials, in cement or other fixatives in such fashion as to produce a surface design. Mosaics are usually attached to a flat surface.

1. Mayer, Ralph. "The Artist's Handbook of Materials and Techniques," The Viking Press, New York, 1940. Pgs. 278-9.

TECHNICAL HIGH SCHOOL, OMAHA, NEBRASKA, MRS. BETTE SANDBOURNE, TEACHER

Omaha, Nebraska, celebrated the Nebraska Territorial Centennial in 1954. Historical events such as the Blizzard of '88, the Grasshopper Scourge, Grass Fires, and Easter Tornado of 1913 were depicted in a library mural by the Technical High School Art Department. Charcoal sketches were cut into sections, traced on white canvas, and painted with silk screen paint. With only red, yellow, blue, green and white, the wide range of colors had to be mixed on the palettes. Pint jars with lids were filled with colors to facilitate setting up the palettes and avoid opening the cans any more than necessary. The mural was completed in nine weeks.

ST. JOHN'S HIGH SCHOOL, WINNIPEG, MANITOBA, CANADA, MISS DAISY BAIG, TEACHER

"Costumes Through the Ages" covers a wall space of 27 by 4 feet in St. John's High School, Winnipeg, Manitoba, Canada. After the theme was chosen, students chose the periods which interested them most. This required considerable research. Small preliminary sketches were made, then enlarged, together with color schemes. The mural was painted in three sections, on wallboard, with household enamel to give a smooth, shiny, permanent finish. In this photograph we see the mural on display at Hudson's Bay Company in Winnipeg.

Illustrations were selected from about 1,000 drawings by elementary children in Marylin Avenue School, Livermore, California. Original illustrations of "Products and Industries of California" were enlarged by using an opaque projector and then the child making the original drawing colored this enlargement. This was transferred to the 6- x 8-inch copper plates by tracing over the enlarged drawing using carbon paper between it and the plates. The plates were etched, enameled with procelain enamels, fired and mounted. All enameling was done by fifth and sixth grade children under the supervision of Mr. Giblin, Principal, and Mrs. Marjorie Kelley, Art Supervisor.

The subject for the permanent mural should be considered very carefully and be appropriate for the space, room, and purpose for which it is created. Some suggested subjects might be the history of the community, depicting local industries, educational and industrial achievements, honoring a community citizen, the heraldry of the school, special subjects for particular rooms such as music subjects for the music room. It should be a mural of which people will not tire. For example, over a period of time people may tire of humorous or political murals.

Older students may enjoy studying famous murals of the world to determine the type of subjects that have endured through the centuries. In the larger communities, murals found in public buildings and banks may also suggest the type that is appropriate for the community. In the Southwest the simple Indian motif of painting has proven very adaptable to the adobe type of architecture, while in the northern states the beauty of the lumber, stone, or brick structures may suggest an entirely different type of subject.

Enameling murals on sheet steel, copper, iron, silver, and aluminum has been developed and featured in United States since 1933 by Edward Winter. He introduced the use of lump and string textures for accents, silver foil for luminous effects, the application technique of sifting powdered enamel onto the metal base, and other techniques.

Upper right:
A 164-foot mosaic and plaster mural depicting the history of music through the ages extends above the foyer of the exterior of the University of California, Los Angeles (UCLA), Music Building. The mural was designed by Richard Haines, Head of the Painting Department of the Los Angeles County Art Institute and installed by the Havenna Company of St. Louis.

Lower right:
The south wall of the reception lobby on the fourth floor of the Welton Becket and Associates Building in Los Angeles faces a beige precast concrete block mural. Cast in sand, it is 9 feet high and 30 feet long. Designed by John Smith, the mural is titled "The Trojan Horse."

Lower left:
Reuben Nakian's huge aluminum facade sculpture consists of fifteen 6- by 3-foot rectangles curved and bent to suggest swirling leaves or birds in flight.

NEW YORK UNIVERSITY LOEB STUDENT CENTER FACADE SCULPTURE BY REUBEN NAKIAN.
PHOTO BY STANLEY SELIGSON

TEMPORARY MURALS

The temporary mural is usually created for special occasions or purposes and may be easily removed and replaced. This type of mural makes an important contribution to the school curriculum because of its current interest feature.

The temporary mural may be made with simple sketches or painted directly on the surface. With this type of mural it may not be necessary to go into much detail, allowing more flexibility to make changes during the process of execution. Such a procedure is in keeping with the environment and the purpose for which it is made.

Special events that may be featured are: Halloween, Thanksgiving, Christmas, Valentine's Day, Easter, Fourth of July, festivals, carnivals, circuses, sports, pioneer days, western days, dedication days, Arbor Day.

APPLETON PUBLIC SCHOOLS, APPLETON, WISCONSIN, DEAN CASWELL, TEACHER

The return of a trip to a neighboring community, a fair, circus, or other place of interest is always an invitation to retrace one's steps in the form of a mural.

BALTIMORE PUBLIC SCHOOLS, BALTIMORE, MARYLAND

2

Creating the School Mural

Creating a school mural provides an opportunity for group expression. It is usually a cooperative enterprise involving the search for facts, planning, organizing, and executing. "Every participant subordinates his own contribution to the whole, yet all have the feeling of cooperative accomplishment," states Viktor Lowenfeld in "Creative and Mental Growth."[1]

Whether the mural is made in correlation with other school subjects or as a separate art project, it is valuable as a means of teaching self-expression, cooperation, and appreciation. By creating murals, children's interest in school life and in activities is increased. The classroom that displays murals made by its pupils is a warm friendly place where children like to work.

CHOOSING A SUBJECT

An opportune time to decide on a subject for a mural is when a situation arises from daily activities of the children which requires the use of creative art. One of the main objectives of the art education program is to help children experience the fact that art is an integral part of everyday life, not a thing apart.

The idea of making a mural may come from the children themselves. When ideas present themselves, recognize and capitalize on them. A teacher should guide their thinking and may list the suggestions the children make on the chalkboard. As a member of the group, the teacher may add one or two of his own ideas along with the children's.

1. Lowenfeld, Viktor. "Creative and Mental Growth," The Macmillan Company, New York, 1947. Pg. 206.

There are many important, everyday experiences of children which are appropriate for mural activities. Personal interests and group experiences almost always stimulate creative expression. Children's reactions to the world about them offer an appeal to the imagination. A mural may be a spontaneous outgrowth of an exciting adventure. Children thoroughly enjoy reliving a circus or carnival that comes to town. Science field trips provide numerous interesting mural projects. Excursions to a bakery, post office, train depot, docks, factories, farms, hospitals, sports events are but a few of the many places available for almost every class to visit.

Choosing a subject may grow out of:
1. A group art activity just for the fun of doing it.
2. Topics suggested by the class.
3. Other subjects or projects in the curriculum.
4. A need for a large cooperative project or a series of related pictures.
5. The need for students to participate and share experiences in a group activity.

The subject for the mural should be shared, discussed, and enthusiastically felt by the teacher and children before starting. After discussions, with all children participating, their own thoughts and feelings will develop and create a mood for doing the mural. Murals started immediately following trips, a play, or story are more meaningful than work attempted after a long period of time has elapsed.

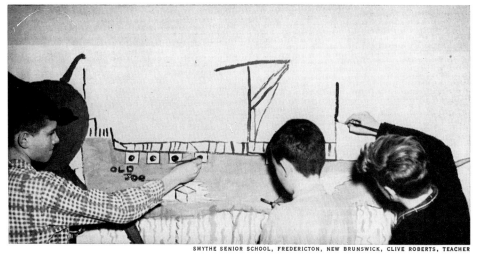

SMYTHE SENIOR SCHOOL, FREDERICTON, NEW BRUNSWICK, CLIVE ROBERTS, TEACHER

A large blank piece of paper was placed over the chalkboard with masking tape. It helped children visualize what they wanted to paint or draw. When it was time to choose a subject for the mural, it was not a problem of building up a subject, but rather one of selecting. These boys decided to depict a story of the seas.

PLANNING

The success of the mural often lies in the teacher's carefully organized planning before the children begin work. These plans should be flexible so that they may be altered to fit the needs of the mural as the activity progresses. It is also the teacher's responsibility to motivate and direct the children's interest, imagination, and cooperation. Together the teacher and children plan the activity. The teacher encourages the children to make decisions for themselves and helps them to observe and discover interesting facts as well as decide what to include in the mural. The ideas expressed in the mural should be based on the children's own experiences, knowledge, and observa-

27

tion. The teacher is primarily concerned with the way he can help pupils become better individuals. Since a mural activity may be one of the ways through which he can achieve this, he keeps in mind the individual differences and interests of the children and encourages them to express their experiences in a creative and unrestrained manner rather than being concerned with the finished product.

With older children the history of murals may be discussed and viewed through pictures. By taking trips to museums or buildings that feature murals, pupils may observe interesting and different types of murals and the application of various techniques and media. This will help give them ideas for their own murals.

ARRANGING COMMITTEES

Committees can play an important role in the making of a mural. Groups or committees may be formed by the children themselves, each committee assuming the responsibility for one phase of the mural. A leader may be selected by the group if one is needed. Small groups or teams do not always need a leader. Through group discussions each child can decide what he would like to do and the type of committee on which he would like to serve. When everyone wants to work on the same thing, some system of fair allotment may be necessary.

Responsibilities of each committee may be written on the chalkboard in order that everyone will know his particular duties. Some of the group responsibilities might be:

1. An information group to check the accuracy of facts used.
2. A group to arrange for a suitable display space in the classroom or another part of the school building.
3. Teams to measure and cut the paper.
4. A committee to do the figures on the mural.
5. A committee to develop the background.
6. A committee to be responsible for the collecting, distributing, and storage of art materials.
7. A group to put the mural in its proper place.
8. A group to plan a follow-up of the mural project, such as
   a. For parents and friends to visit the school
   b. For class discussion
   c. To arrange for visits from other rooms
   d. To display the mural in a business district
   e. To arrange a television or radio program
   f. To write a school newspaper article on the mural activity
9. A committee to study the music or dramatic relationships to be used with the mural project.
10. A story to be written to explain the significance of the mural, such as the story of Daniel Boone's explorations.

MAKING THE MURAL

After the subject for the mural has been chosen, a class needs to decide on the medium and type of background paper it wishes to use. The mural project should be of a type and size that can be completed in a reasonable time before children tire of the activity. Before undertaking a new project, some teachers advise discussing and evaluating previous mural activities.

A mural activity in the primary grades will differ somewhat from one in the upper grades. No matter what grade, however, the activity may be developed in ways that encourage exploration in various media, develop increased art knowledge and skill, and allow for creative experiences through a variety of activities.

Young Children

Murals in the kindergarten or primary groups are simple. While there are many ways of arriving at a mural activity, ideas are almost always initiated through discussion so that children can share in the planning. Ideas will materialize through discussion, perhaps stimulated by such means as dramatic plays, records, and field trips.

Since pupils tend to do the things they can do the best, their interests should be broadened to include different materials and a variety of subjects so they will have incentive for improving their skills.

Next they will decide where to put the mural, how large they wish it to be, and what material to use to portray their experiences. Most old classrooms are equipped with an abundance of chalkboard space which may be used for chalk murals or covered with large strips of paper for the background of a mural. The challenge is to make it look like one big panel rather than many small drawings. By discussing the experience they plan to depict on this large paper, children learn to work together for a common goal. Since some young children are not accustomed to working together, especially the first part of the year, it is usually advisable for each one to be given a specific space in which to work.

To maintain a high level of interest, the teacher may want to alternate work on the mural with group discussions. From these the pupils will decide whether to fill in empty spaces or in some other way to make the mural look like one big border and not small separate pictures. The teacher may ask: Are the figures large enough? Can everyone see them? Do they fill the space? Are the larger figures in the front and the smaller ones in the background? If there is a tendency for the children to draw small pinched drawings, the teacher can suggest that figures extend from the top to the bottom of the paper.

It is the teacher's responsibility to keep the spirit of the mural activity informal, relaxed, and uninhibited. The interest span of younger children is very short. Their murals should be simple, easy to make, and capable of completion in a relatively short time. When their expression is no longer enthusiastic and spontaneous, it is time to stop.

Second grade children enjoy painting together on a group picture.

Chalk is a flexible medium. If a child wishes to alter any portion of his work it can be erased and a fresh start made. The flexibility of chalk on paper is much the same as it is on chalkboard. Many teachers are discouraging the use of the pencil for "sketching in" as children tend to draw small pinched figures with pencils. Some teachers have found it particularly valuable to work directly in the medium rather than filling in sketches made with an unrelated medium. (See Chapter III, page 48.)

Crayon is one of the media that can be used in coloring a mural. There are innumerable ways of stimulating variation and originality with crayon. (See Chapter III, page 46.)

If children's experiences have been limited to pencil and crayon, the transition to painting with brushes may be easily made by using inch squares of plastic sponge on newspapers. This encourages the child to express himself freely in large figures and to learn the relationship of blended colors. Even though he may get paint on his hands, it will wash off easily with soap and water. The objects and forms young children paint may be symbolic, simple, direct, and flat without form or perspective. They tend to paint with bold, free movements. This is as it should be.

Children in the lower grades should have freedom in choosing colors. However, some may be influenced by their friend's choice unless there is a discussion regarding colors. (See Chapter 1, page 10.)

Children enjoy the economical and easy-to-handle poster and powder paints. Each child works differently with paints, usually according to his experiences. Some pupils paint in timid strokes; others splash paint over the entire piece of paper; some paint in spots of colors; still others paint on just one small area.

Young children usually make simple backgrounds of sky, sun, moon, water, ground. As they acquire more experience their backgrounds become more important and include many more details. Children usually know what they want and should be encouraged to express their own ideas. After the main mural theme has been created, it may be necessary for the teacher to discuss ways that the background can be related to the main objects.

Black and white silhouettes can also be a lot of fun. The background of the mural is measured and cut to proper size. The cutouts may be temporarily pinned on the mural paper to be evaluated for arrangement. When they are in the desired positions they are ready to be glued or fastened to the mural paper. Background details may be added as needed.

In one school a little girl discovered that if her companions stood still she could draw their entire shadows. The teacher felt this provided for variation in the art activity since the children enjoyed it. This idea stimulated such an interest that teachers, maintenance men, and classmates wanted to pose for their silhouettes. The silhouettes were drawn, cut out, and placed on the chalkboard with the name of the person above the drawing. The social significance of a project of this type can be of value to the school.

Children in another school discovered that when they walked in front of a slide projector, a crisp shadow was cast on the screen. They found they could make exact likenesses of each other by projecting the shadow and drawing around it on a large piece of white paper which was tacked to the wall.

In reviewing the history of mosaic murals it has been discovered that items such as colored stones, broken glass, crockery, or ceramic ware were used. Children may follow very much the same practice, using the materials they have in school or home. Colored paper, colored pages of magazines, cloth, or similar items may be torn or cut into shapes, arranged, and pasted on paper. Such articles as buttons, stones, sea shells, plastic may be cemented to a plywood or masonite base with a good household cement or tile mastic. (See Chapter III, page 56.)

Children like to label a piece of work. Lettering may be used as part of the design as well as to tell the story. To be a part of the design, the lettering must give contrast to other parts of the mural as well as fit the general pattern. The lettering may be done with crayons, paints, or cutout paper letters.

FOSTER ELEMENTARY SCHOOL, HOUSTON, TEXAS, MARTHA C. BARNETTE, TEACHER

Teachers have found that cutout paper figures for murals are satisfactory for most young children since much of the work can be done at desks or tables with every child sharing the responsibilities. The students in the above picture did easel paintings of animals; cut out the animals and pasted them on brown wrapping-paper background. Green wrapping paper was shredded and pasted on, making a lower border of "grass" for the completed mural.

COURTESY ALAMEDA COUNTY SCHOOLS, HAYWARD, CALIFORNIA

Aluminum foil was used by a primary class to create this mural.

32

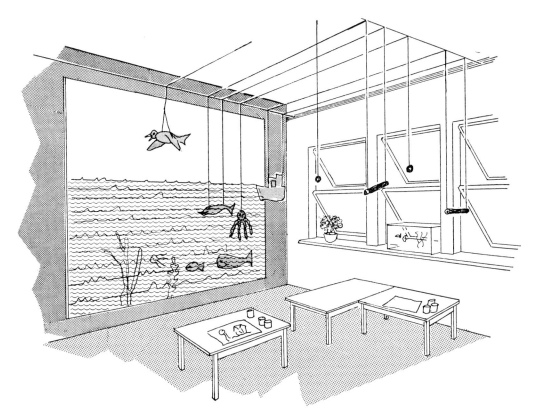

PUPPET MURAL

The third grade students at F Street School, Chula Vista, California, decided to make a mural after visiting the tide pool to observe the sea, animals, and plant life. The back of the room was covered with butcher paper 7 feet high. Committees were formed to plan, cut, paste, paint, and study sea animals. Children thought it would be fun to make animals in the mural move. Sides of the animals were painted on two pieces of butcher paper, cut out, stuffed with newspaper, and stapled together. Two strings were attached to the animals and tied to erasers. The erasers were thrown over a 16-gauge wire fastened to the molding above the mural with a screw eye, and on the other side with a turn-buckle and screw eye. The erasers were thrown over a wire stretched at the other end of the room. Erasers were removed and strings attached to a small rod. When an animal was controlled by one string a metal washer was tied to the end of the string and slipped over a tack to keep it in place. Children learned to control the animals 30 feet away by manipulating the rod. The animals in motion stirred the class to further creativity and original songs were composed by the children.

A mural is displayed in the showcase in the corridor of Wheelock Elementary School, Lubbock, Texas.

In a scribble mural the challenge of free lines and shapes stimulates children's imaginations. Each child adds a triangle, square, circle, or other shape. When all children have contributed, a center of interest is outlined. Colored tempera paints or chalks enhance the scribble mural.

WAHL-COATES LABORATORY SCHOOL, EAST CAROLINA COLLEGE, GREENVILLE, NORTH CAROLINA

On a large sheet of white butcher paper second graders drew animals, trees and foliage. Since the class was learning to measure feet and inches in arithmetic, they measured and drew the mural into foot squares. These were numbered, cut and colored. The squares were then arranged according to number and pasted to another sheet of butcher paper.

WHEELOCK ELEMENTARY SCHOOL, LUBBOCK, TEXAS, MRS. ELEANOR BOWLING, TEACHER

Older Pupils

Children of the upper grades have usually had previous experiences in creative activities and their approach is more purposeful. Teachers at all levels use relatively the same methods of achieving their objectives, forming committees, arranging for materials, and carrying out the details of the mural activity. The methods used by the teacher of older pupils may vary with the personality of the teacher and the interests of the children.

To add to children's experiences, an opaque projector can be used to "blow up" small drawings or sketches to the size needed for large murals. The drawings to be projected should be outlined with a dark heavy crayon line so they will project clearly. Before projecting the sketch, the projector should be arranged for distances and the room darkened, if necessary.

A 2- by 3-inch lantern slide projector may also be used. First the pupils make their drawings on tracing paper the size of a slide. The drawing is placed between glass slides. The slide is then placed in the projector and the picture focused on the mural background. The pupils then trace the enlarged image. They are now ready to paint.

All children should share in enlarging a sketch for a mural at some time. A committee may be chosen to sketch the larger mural directly on wrapping paper and submit it to the class for approval. Drawing on wrapping paper may be done with chalk or charcoal, but preferably not with pencil as it tends to make the work too small. Chalk and charcoal are flexible, quick, easy to erase for corrections, and offer wide

CHICAGO PUBLIC SCHOOLS, CHICAGO, ILLINOIS

Murals may be planned in several ways. Pupils may want to make a number and variety of sketches for preliminary planning and discussing. After the class discussion in one class, all pupils drew small sketches and chose the one desired for the mural. Another class took various parts from several sketches and combined them into a new composition. Still another class formed groups with each pupil making original sketches. Each group then submitted sketches to the class for consideration and additional suggestions.

35

opportunity for blending and shading. Some prefer to sketch only the basic outlines of the composition, leaving the details for the final work. Charcoal being black means care must be used to prevent soiling the floor, walls, and clothing. The same is true of colored chalk. Children should be encouraged to wear old shirts, smocks, aprons, and overalls while working on the mural.

Upper grade children are interested in specific colors and color combinations. This will provide for color study and usage. (See Chapter I, page 10.)

Most children should share in painting the details, background, lettering, and border. They can take turns being responsible for mixing the paint, washing the brushes, or performing other activities related to the project. Placing the paper on the floor makes painting easy and satisfactory. By working on the floor no ladders are needed, thus the danger of accidents is minimized.

Cutout murals for older pupils are approached in the same manner as those for younger children. The class may share in the general planning procedure with each student submitting his cutout for placement. They may be rearranged until the desired composition is obtained.

Textured and colored papers, yarns, cloth, wire, and miscellaneous items such as seeds, pods, sea shells, vegetables, stones, may be used to make mosaic as well as three-dimensional murals. (See Chapter III, page 56.)

PETER PAN SCHOOL, DENVER, COLORADO, ED KIRCHNER, ART TEACHER

After suggested changes in arrangement, composition, and lettering have been discussed and agreed upon, drawings for the entire mural may be sketched, according to scale, on the large mural paper. Each square across the top of the mural is numbered and alphabet letters are used down the side of the page. When an enlargement or reduction is desired, one need only to stay within the squares.

36

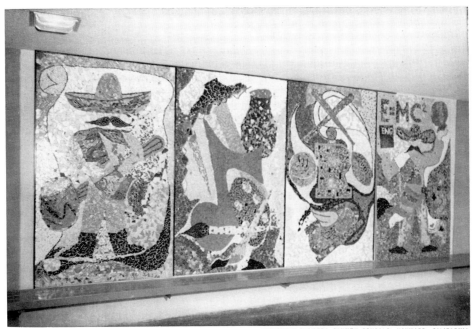

The Academic Panels created at the Rancho Arroyo School in Hayward, under the supervision of Emi Luptak, are comprised of different types of tiles, shells, and marble chips.

HOUSTON PUBLIC SCHOOLS, HOUSTON, TEXAS, NORMA LYNN WOOD, TEACHER

An entire Christmas party was planned for the interests of younger children. A high school art class arranged Christmas elf masks against the walls of their studio room. They worked in teams of two, one placing a square of metal foil over his own face, with eyes closed, and the other acting as an assistant to help in slowly molding the contours of the face. Wet strips of paper coated with wheat paste were placed in successive layers directly over the metal foil. When dry they were painted with tempera paint. The junior high school art class made hands for the elves in the same manner. Elementary students made feet for the elves by rolling and tying newspaper to form a variation of a capital "L." Strips of papier-mâché were applied over this. When dry they were painted to match the head and hands. Strips of construction paper were stapled to the heads, hands, and feet to make the bodies.

HOW TO FASTEN THE MURAL

Fastening the mural to the wall should be done with care. Secure the approval of the principal before using gummed paper, cellulose tape, masking tape, adhesive tape, thumbtacks, paste, or glue to hold a paper mural to a wall since some will peel the paint and others will leave gummy discoloration that is difficult to remove.

Wallboard, masonite, and plywood murals may be raised to a higher elevation by fastening two pulleys to either the ceiling or wall. Through the pulleys, light but strong rope is run and attached to a board on which the mural is securely fastened. It can then be raised and suspended at the desired height above the floor. The loose end of the rope is fastened to a cleat in an inconspicuous place. It might be advisable for the principal to have workmen do this to prevent injuries.

If considering a permanent mural, consult authorities in mural work as well as architects to assure proper hanging.

WHY WE DO IT?

Educators feel that all learning experiences are valuable and that evaluation is essential in some phases of learning. As the mural progresses it may be necessary for the teacher and children to determine what they are deriving from their experience. Teachers are becoming increasingly aware of the importance of art experiences in the over-all development of children rather than the attainment of a product. However, a mural activity may have been chosen to fill a specific purpose, in which event the teacher and pupils may wish to evaluate the activity.

If the objective was purely to give experience in the use of materials, then a review and discussion would be sufficient to establish in the minds of the youngsters the experiences gained through the use of these materials. If the objectives were to relate the art activities with other areas of learning, the teacher may want to analyze with the youngsters as they work on the mural how well they are reaching their aims. If the mural developed out of a social need within the class the teacher may find it advisable not to discuss with the class the particular social problems he had hoped to correct. However, he may want to praise certain youngsters for their willingness to cooperate. If the objective was to develop the perceptual powers of youngsters, the composition might be discussed in relation to similar objects.

The teacher may wish to evaluate the importance and objectives of the project for himself:

1. Do I provide for individual interests and abilities?
2. Do my pupils have a variety of materials and free choice in selecting them? Are the materials readily available?
3. Do I try to incorporate into the project as many of the arts and skills and other areas of learning as the children really need for the particular art activity in which they are engaged?
4. Do the children feel free to express their creative ideas when they wish?
5. Are the children relaxed and enjoying the project? Are any frustrated? How can I help them without adding to their annoyance?
6. Is the project within the experiences and knowledge of the class?
7. Do I use community resources when they can be helpful?
8. Do I use films and other visual aids on the subjects involved in the project when their use is indicated?
9. Do I take my class on excursions related to the project?
10. Are there a variety of activities so every child has an opportunity to enjoy at least one?
11. Have I improved the children's standards of good taste, ability to detect art quality, and appreciation of beauty in surroundings?
12. Do I help children improve their art skills without imposing techniques?
13. Does the mural help expand their other art interests?

40

A few of the items a class may wish to evaluate regarding the mechanics of the mural are:

1. Is the original plan being followed?
2. Does the mural fill the space well?
3. Are the colors appropriate?
4. Are the areas interesting?   Are there both large and small objects?
5. Does the mural need strong border interests?
6. Does the background fit the theme?

Students of Rancho Arroyo School eagerly watch the transformation of a white wall into four panels alive with rhythms of color.

AFTER THE MURAL, THEN WHAT?

It is hoped that the learning which took place during the process of making the mural will be more important than the completed mural.   However, if the mural was made for a specific reason, then this fact should be recognized.

On a few occasions recognition may be made of the mural project.   Parents and friends may be invited to the unveiling.   Sponsoring business organizations may share in the ceremonies. The local radio, television, or newspaper may wish to feature the

41

mural. A local department store may be invited to use it as a window display. A story in the school paper may be used to arouse interest from the student body.

Most teachers feel that no one individual's work should be recognized to the exclusion of the group. If one child is pointed out as the "artist" the others may feel their participation was not worthy of recognition.

Since a mural is considered a group activity, demonstrations of making a mural will invariably attract more attention than the final product. Some teachers have found it worthwhile to invite the parents to watch progress during construction since many parents never visit the classroom, and the art education of their children depends largely on the few drawings and pieces of creative work they bring home.

A short television show depicting the various steps in making a mural can be an interesting demonstration on parents' night. The several steps in planning and constructing the mural can be grouped in the television studio with the camera moving from one group to the other, reconstructing each step for the television audience.

STORAGE OF MURALS

Sometimes it is necessary for the teacher to store a mural for future use. Long murals may be rolled and stored in large mailing tubes or boxes of appropriate type and size. It may be necessary to store long flat pieces between the wall and filing cabinets unless the classroom has adequate drawer space. Canvas or cloth murals should be stored on original stretchers, protected by plywood or building board backing to prevent damage. A framed canvas mural should be suspended by eye screws fastened into the frame to prevent sagging from the weight of the paint. An unframed canvas mural may be rolled if the paint does not tend to crack. Plywood and masonite murals are the strongest and least subject to damage. However, it is advisable to store them in a vertical position, against the wall on blocks of wood and, if possible, behind the protection of filing cases. Murals of cardboard should have the same protection from possible damage as those of canvas or other fabrics.

A mural produced by children can be an inspirational background to stimulate creativity among adults in other art activities.

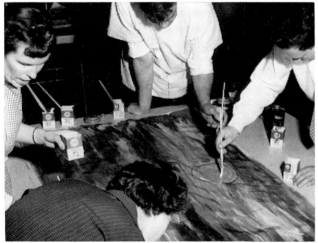

By working together teachers develop an appreciation for some of the problems children may have in mural production.

43

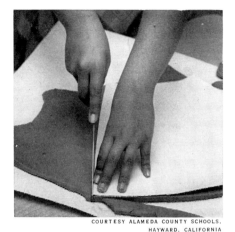

3

COURTESY ALAMEDA COUNTY SCHOOLS,
HAYWARD, CALIFORNIA

Materials to Use

If a variety of materials and media are provided, children will find a way to use them. Boys and girls should be encouraged to explore and to experiment with the various art materials available in order to gain experience in their uses. It is the teacher's responsibility to guide and to assist in learning new uses and handling different types of media.

Children should learn to understand the potentialities and limitations of each medium. Also, learning an art vocabulary can be fun if it is limited to words that are natural for children. Demonstrations before the class can be helpful but should, if possible, involve at least some of the children and never be too long and verbal. Occasionally a period to just play with materials may be educational and interesting. During such periods the teacher learns about the children's interests. A teacher should:

1. Experiment with materials before they are made available to children.
2. Learn potentialities and limitations of art materials.
3. Demonstrate if asked to do so, but assure pupils that there are a number of ways of doing each activity.
4. Use a large variety of materials.
5. Praise some phase of each student's work.
6. Provide work corners or art tables where children may have access to art material at all times.
7. Procure and display murals from other schools and sources.
8. Avoid duplicated outlines.

9. Find out where to go for assistance and reference materials.

10. Secure service from specialists. They are usually willing to help.

11. Avoid drawing on children's work. Have paper available on which to demonstrate.

12. Have children draw or paint together occasionally. Art is a sharing of experiences.

13. Take advantage of all visual aid materials possible. Know the sources.

14. The project is that of children; the teacher only directs and guides.

15. Understand children's many interests and experiences.

16. Send information to parents explaining the objectives of the mural so they may cooperate in attaining the proper results.

17. Exhibit art work whenever an opportunity presents itself.

18. Smile.

A GUIDE FOR USE OF MATERIALS
CRAYONS (wax)
Basic Materials

1. Crayons (wax). Large wax crayon is desirable for kindergarten and first grade pupils. Some teachers prefer 6–8 stick color boxes for younger children and 16–24 stick color boxes for older pupils.

2. Paper or cloth.

3. Knife.

Method

1. Crayons may be applied on paper, cloth, wood, or other textured surfaces. Crayons will damage walls and chalkboards.

2. The side of crayon may be used for tone, blocking in, or wide lines; the point for sharp, clear lines or detail.

3. Crayons may be pressed firmly onto the paper to make work rich and brilliant. Broken pieces may be used flat against the paper to vary effects and designs.

4. Interest may be achieved by using crayon on colored paper and by the blending of colored chalks.

5. Variations of lights and darks will result by applying unequal pressure.

6. Interesting lettering may be done by using the side of crayons.

7. To produce good contrast, dark colors may be applied next to light colors.

8. Notches may be cut on the side of crayon with scissors or fingernails. This will produce a striped effect in coloring, create plaid or surface patterns, or indicate line directions.

9. Wavy, straight, curved, zigzag, spiral, or other patterns may be created by holding the side of crayon flat against the paper and changing the amount of pressure or line direction.

10. To smooth the color and give a glossy surface, a finger, stump (a hard twisted paper for blending the colors), or eraser may be rubbed vigorously over the colored surface.

Variations

1. For interesting texture, water-color paints, ink, or tempera paint may be applied to crayon drawing with a brush or sponge.
2. Children may desire to do crayon etching. A solid light color is applied to the paper. This is covered with a second darker color. With a sharp instrument, such as point of scissors, fingernail, hairpin, bobby pin, the artist draws a design on the darker color, thus exposing the lighter color.
3. Crayon may be melted in a container submerged in a pan of warm water. The melted crayon may be applied with a brush like paint.
4. For good textural variations, paper may be placed over sandpaper, string, screen wire, corrugated paper, cloth, leather and then colored with crayon.
5. Crayon designs may be drawn directly on cloth. The colors may be set by placing the cloth between newspapers and pressing with a warm iron. Care should be taken to prevent the material from slipping while being pressed.
6. One part broken crayons may be dissolved in two parts turpentine. This mixture may be painted on cloth and pressed with a hot iron. When painted on paper it dries quickly without ironing.
7. A heavy crayon design may be drawn on paper, leaving background areas uncolored. Crush paper after it has been quickly dipped in water. Drop tempera or water colors on the surface of the smoothed-out crushed paper. The crayon will resist the paint, only the uncolored areas will take the paint.
8. Crayons may be used on stencils. For added interest, cut out geometric as well as other designs. Use both the positive and negative parts of the stencil in combinations.

Care

1. Trampled crayons will cause damage to most floors. Keep them in a box or can.
2. Crayons will melt if placed on a radiator or near excessive heat.
3. By keeping a small pad of paper on the crayon storage shelf, children may test the colors.
4. Crayon marks may be removed with turpentine, solvent, naptha, or cleaning fluids. Check with the principal before using any inflammable solvents so as to comply with local fire regulations.

To Make Crayon Drawings Permanent

1. A wax crayon drawing may be heated so the colors will be impregnated into the fiber to become more durable.

2. Crayon designs on wood, wallboard, or tagboard may be painted with shellac, clear lacquer, or any of several different types of waxes or polishes.

CHALK

Basic Materials

1. Chalkboard colors, lecturer's chalk, pastels.
2. Paper or chalkboard
3. Stump, a hard twisted paper for blending colors.
4. Felt chalkboard erasers, cloth, rubber sponge, shammy, or regular pencil eraser.
5. Water-color brush.

Method

1. For greater coverage the side of chalk may be used. Details or finishing marks may be added last by using the end of the chalk.
2. Even though chalk is a softer medium than wax crayon, it may be used much the same way.
3. Experiment with chalk for interesting variations.
4. Interesting color combinations and smooth blended effects may be secured by blending two or more colors on the paper with a piece of cloth, fingers, or stump. Avoid too much rubbing lest the quality of colors be lost.
5. Varying amounts of pressure in chalk drawing may be used to add intensity.

Variations

1. Chalk may be combined with other media to make effective murals.
2. Paper may be moistened with a sponge and the illustration drawn directly on it with chalk. This increases the intensity of the color. The tip of the chalk may be dipped in water to obtain similar results.
3. For a substitute, tempera paint may be made by pulverizing chalk and adding a little mucilage. Older children may make an "oil paint" by pulverizing the chalk and stirring in clear varnish. This may be applied with a bristle brush for results almost comparable to regular oil paint.
4. Powdered chalk may be made by rubbing colored chalk against a piece of sandpaper or other rough surface, or scraping with a knife. This powder may be applied to paintings or drawings with a sponge, cotton, or piece of cloth very much like tempera paint.
5. Pulverized chalk may be added to a starch finger paint base. Additional chalk may be added to increase intensity of color desired. Paper to be used may be a determining factor in the thickness of the starch. Experiment with finger paint before starting to paint.
6. Lacquer may be added to powdered chalk to make a relatively fast color for textile painting or stenciling. Lacquer thinner will need to be added regularly since lacquer dries very rapidly.
7. By placing a piece of paper over a textured surface and drawing with chalk, the texture may be transferred to the paper.

8. With a thumbtack fasten a piece of string to a board; place a piece of paper on the board and under the string. Coat string with colored chalk. Hold loose end of string at other end of paper so it is tight. Snap middle of string to release powdered chalk to paper. The string may be moved at different angles on the paper to give a variety of patterns.

Care

1. Colored chalk may be stored in small boxes to keep it clean.
2. Wrap paper or masking tape around chalk for a holder to help keep hands clean.
3. Before using chalk, apply a light film of soap to hands. Allow the hands to dry. When hands are moistened again the soap will dissolve, washing away the chalk stains.
4. Some teachers use an atomizer to keep paper slightly dampened. A few drops of glycerine reduces the evaporation and dust formed by chalk.
5. To protect clothing, wear an apron, smock, or old shirt.
6. Sweep or vacuum dust rather than pick it up with wet rags.

Fixatives

1. Chalk may be set with a fixative. This may be purchased commercially or made by combining 90% alcohol and 10% white shellac. Other recipes for fixatives are: five parts of wood alcohol to one part white shellac; five parts methyl alcohol to one part shellac. Colored shellac darkens colors. Some commercial fixatives come with blowers. An inexpensive ten-cent store spray gun may be used for spraying.

ELLENSBURG PUBLIC SCHOOLS, ELLENSBURG, WASHINGTON

New ways of using chalk will prompt children to adapt the design to the medium.

49

2. School paste, mucilage, or other water-soluble adhesives, thinned with water to a milklike consistency are satisfactory fixatives and inexpensive. Another type of fixative is a thin solution of gum arabic mixed with water. One should experiment before applying it to art work that is to be kept permanently.

TEMPERA OR POSTER PAINTS AND WATER COLORS
Basic Materials

1. Tempera or poster paints are available in liquid and powdered form. Others may have mucilage added to them and classified as casein paints. These may be considered opaque water-soluble paints. Water colors either in the cake form or in tubes may not be used as extensively on murals because of their transparent quality.
2. Brushes, cotton, sponge. For younger children the teacher may want a brush for each color or a brush for each child. Large brushes are most satisfactory for younger children; medium for older pupils.
3. Paper, chalkboard, cloth, cardboard.
4. Paint rags for cleaning.
5. Pans, muffin tins, tin cans, aluminum tin-foil plates, or dinner plates for paints and water.
6. Aprons, smocks, or old shirts for clothing protection.
7. Pan or bucket of water for washing hands and arms if other wash facilities are not available.
8. Newspapers to work on and for finished work to dry on.

Method for Wet Tempera

1. A tempera paint mural may be painted on a variety of papers or chalkboard. A chalkboard mural may be washed off since tempera paint is soluble in water. Check with school principal to be sure that the type of chalkboard in the school lends itself to tempera.
2. Experiment with a brush to learn a variety of techniques.
3. By painting on paper which has been thoroughly dampened, colors may blend more freely. Details may be added after it has begun to dry.
4. Painting with a sponge or piece of cotton in place of a brush creates interesting effects.

Method for Dry Tempera

1. Powdered paint is available in most school supply stores. Add enough water to dry tempera to form a creamy consistency and soak about 5 minutes before using. Some powdered paints may be mixed with water at the moment of use. It is important that powdered tempera be mixed to the proper consistency depending on the paper to be used. It is advisable to experiment with the tempera and paper before starting to paint. Paints should be checked for toxic impurities.

50

Selecting and mixing the right amounts of paint can be a group responsibility.

This committee of students is painting the background of their Southwest Indian mural with tempera paints. The bold quality of tempera lends itself to large free expression.

2. Powdered calcimine serves as many uses in the classroom as tempera paints. It may also be purchased by the pound. It is mixed the same as tempera paints. Calcimine paints should be checked for toxic impurities.

3. Encourage children to mix their own colors in order to find desired color combinations.

Variations for Wet or Dry Tempera

1. To make paint stick more readily to a surface, honey, mucilage, or paste may be added.

2. Textile paint may be added to dry tempera to make a fast textile color. Follow the instructions of the manufacturer.

3. Varnish and dry tempera may be mixed to make an oil paint.

4. Drawing with paraffine may serve as a resist, thus introducing light lines when painting with wet or dry tempera.

5. Tempera added to a finger paint base is a good color medium for silk screen murals. Each child may print a figure on a long piece of paper. The figures may be united by strong base, background or connecting lines.

6. A few drops of different colored tempera may be dropped on a piece of paper. Press second piece of paper over it for interesting blotted patterns.

7. Painting on corrugated paper will give a variety of unusual effects. Painting may be done with or against the ridges, inside, or on top of ridges.

8. Glossy oil paints may be made by mixing powder paint with either clear shellac, lacquer, or varnish instead of water. The more varnish used, the glossier the finish.

9. Tempera may be mixed with various media such as wax crayon, chalk, India ink, or oil paint for unusual results.

Care

1. Keep jars of paint securely covered at all times when not in use. Turn jars end for end regularly to minimize caking of colors. A few drops of water may be added also to paint jars regularly to prevent paint from drying.

2. Glycerine added to tempera paint will reduce drying time.

3. When painting, keep paints stirred well with a stick or spoon. This will reduce the separating in the paint.

4. Keep the mouth and lid of a tempera jar clean to reduce drying and making it easier to remove lid.

5. Thoroughly clean mixing pans and brushes after being used.

6. Smaller quantities of paint in more jars makes painting easier and available to more children.

7. Wintergreen or spirit of cloves may be added to improve the odor.

8. Painted pictures may be dried by hanging them on a line with clothespins, paper clips, or pins; or laying them over a clothes rack. This will keep them off desks, tables, or floor.

9. Powdered pumice or powdered chalk rubbed on smooth paper before painting will improve the adhesive quality of paint on paper.

Fixatives

1. Tempera that is "chalky" may rub off easily and needs to be treated. Spray the drawing with the same fixatives suggested under "chalk."
2. Spraying paper lightly with water will reduce the smudging by increasing the penetration.
3. It is advisable for the teacher to experiment with fixatives before applying it to paper.

PAPER

Basic Materials

1. Drawing paper, craft, butcher, corrugated, wallpaper, newsprint, colored paper, construction, cardboard, or other kinds of paper available.
2. Any type of painting or drawing materials.
3. Background for murals such as paper, bulletin board, chalkboard, screen, or wire.
4. Pins, paste, glue, scotch tape, rubber cement, stapler, thumbtacks, needles, thread, yarn.
5. Scissors or other cutting tools.

Method

1. Cutout or torn-paper projects are excellent for primary grades. They may be pinned, pasted, glued, or tacked to background, and changed and re-arranged for desired results.
2. Children should be encouraged to work with large shapes.
3. Children may experiment with paper to create many fascinating items by manipulating, cutting, tearing, tucking, scoring, snipping, pleating, folding, curling, crushing, rolling, bending, pinning, pasting, stapling. They may also experiment with color harmonies, various weights, and textured papers.
4. Children easily learn to make squares, circles, rectangles, cones, triangles, or other shapes which may be used as basic forms in sculptured or three-dimensional objects.

Variations

1. Simple effective silhouette murals may be made by drawing or painting. The illusion of distance may be created by painting or pasting a cutout picture on a piece of paper. Cover it with a piece of thin, transparent paper. Draw objects to appear in the foreground on the transparent paper.
2. Interesting paper montage murals may be made by tearing or cutting various shapes from colored or textured papers. These may be arranged in a number of ways on a mural background by pasting, gluing, stapling, or pinning.
3. A collage mural may be made by creating three-dimensional paper sculptured objects and geometric shapes. These may be arranged and fastened to form unusual murals.

Papier-mâché masks and a cut-paper background were used to make this "Mask Tree Mural."

ELLENSBURG PUBLIC SCHOOLS, ELLENSBURG, WASHINGTON

FOSTER ELEMENTARY SCHOOL, HOUSTON, TEXAS, MRS. FLORRIE M. HARGRAVE, TEACHER

For this mural each child painted a picture on a large piece of paper of what he wants to be when he grows up. The completed pictures were cut out and tacked to the bulletin board to form an interesting mural.

4. Travel posters, or other unusual posters, may be used to create effective murals. Posters may be cut apart and cutouts arranged to form a mural.

5. Older students may want to substitute the blade of a sharp knife to do paper sculpture. It is advisable to cut on a heavy piece of paper such as cardboard. Preliminary instructions in the safe handling of sharp objects should precede the use of the sharp instrument.

6. Gift boxes, cosmetic boxes, small cartons of molded or pressed paper may suggest creative structures if an effort is made to relate one to the other by: cutting notches and fitting them together; pinning various shaped boxes on bulletin board to make three-dimensional figures; combining portions of boxes that have been cut out; dressing boxes with crepe paper, cloth, or other colored or textured papers.

7. Painting with and against the ridges of corrugated paper may result in entirely different effects. For variation, one color may be used inside the ridges and another on top of the ridges. Secondary students may enjoy painting with airbrush on corrugated paper.

A variety of papers were used to achieve this farm mural. The parts were cut, pasted, or tacked to the heavy paper background.

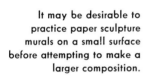

It may be desirable to practice paper sculpture murals on a small surface before attempting to make a larger composition.

CHRIS HARBLE ELEMENTARY SCHOOL, LUBBOCK, TEXAS, MARGARET WAGHORN, TEACHER

This mural was painted on regular newspaper. Children become oblivious of the printing on newspaper and thoroughly enjoy the freedom that old newspapers provide.

8. Wallpaper and sample wallpaper books will provide a good source of material for creative murals.
9. Newspaper is an excellent material on which to paint. Children disregard the printing.

MOSAIC MATERIALS

Basic Materials

1. Items such as seeds, buttons, sea shells, beads, pods, vegetables, plastic, pebbles, marbles, pieces of glass, ceramics, pottery, paper.
2. Background for mosaic mural such as board, cardboard, paper, plywood, masonite.
3. Scissors, knives, pincers, tile clippers, or other cutting instruments, spatula or palette knife.
4. Plaster, sand, cement, mastic, glue, paste, can of adhesive, tile cement (or grout).
5. Container in which to mix plaster or cement.

Method

1. Simple designs may be drawn on paper and filled in with materials to make mosaic murals. Abstract forms, outlined figures of animals, trees, or other objects may be drawn. Arrange items similar in color and form, contrasting them with lighter or darker, larger or smaller pieces. Glue or paste may be used to fasten such items as paper, straws, seeds, pods, and cloth to the mural background.

2. Older children may like to experiment with a variety of challenging materials. They may be interested in trying the following method. Cut a piece of waterproofed plywood or masonite for a base, the size of the project. To minimize warping of the base a clear lacquer may be applied. Outline design or pattern on the base with various color areas labeled.

   Apply items directly to the surface before cementing them. Pieces may be cut and arranged as desired. Tile clippers will cut such items as pottery, ceramic, glass, china, or any flat materials. Cover each piece with a rubber-base adhesive and put in place. Cover only 3 or 4 inches at a time. If a smooth surface is desired, spaces between the pieces may be filled with a tile cement (a process called grouting). Mix cement with water to a consistency of thick cream. This comes in white but may be colored any shade with a dry pigment before adding water. Pour over entire surface and rub gently with a sponge until all crevices between pieces are filled. Remove excess grout with a wet sponge and allow to dry 24 hours. The powdery residue may be wiped off with a damp sponge. When dry, mosaic may be washed with soap and water for a final cleaning. Consult a company which sells mosaic materials for additional advice. Always consult manufacturers on glue, epoxy, or resin for proper adhesives.

Care

1. Clean up plaster or cement before it hardens in the container. Do not pour into a sink.
2. Care should always be exercised when using any sharp materials and instruments.
3. Whenever work described in the second method is stopped for a period, cover finished area with a damp cloth to prevent drying too rapidly and cracking.
4. Keep can of adhesive covered as much of the time as possible to prevent drying.

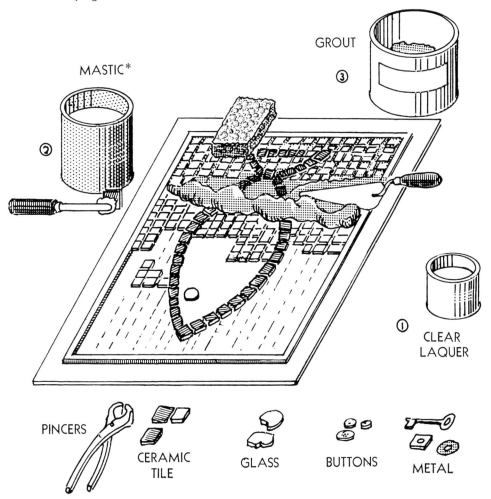

In recent years the popularity of mosaic art has increased. Improved mastics and cements have made it possible for this art to be attempted in schools. The very young may begin with cut-paper mosaics while older children may use with ease regular mosaic materials or find a challenge in materials not common to professional mosaics. It is advisable to begin with a small mosaic.

* Mastic is a quick-setting pasty cement used for adhering tile to a base. It may be purchased from tile concerns and hardware stores.

Joseph L. Young places glass pieces into position with mastic onto the background mural. The center picture is a completed section of the mural which hangs in the Los Angeles Facilities Building, Los Angeles, California. See page 63 for an illustration of the entire mural.

By experimenting first with cut-paper shapes a better understanding will develop for the use of more expensive materials.

More than 200 students at the Junction Avenue School, Livermore, California, under the supervision of Mrs. Marjorie Kelley designed and built a 60-foot mural with 18 ceramic clay life-size figures which depict various phases of an elementary school education. (See dedication pages for other photographs.)

The children's own water fountain murals created under the direction of Mrs. Irene Schulte, Principal, Castro Valley Elementary School, Castro Valley, California, add beauty to the school. Children's pictures were made into composite pictures colored with chalk. From this, children sketched the pictures in pencil on unfired bisque tiles after which ceramic pencils, ceramic chalk, engobe and glaze were applied. Some were fired and then glazed, some glazed and fired at the same time at 2000°F. for three or four hours, then cooled at least 24 hours. One of the fathers installed them with commercial tiles forming the borders.

This mural is being made with salt and flour on an old corrugated packing box. In order to produce contrasts in color, the first layer of salt and flour was colored with tempera paint before being applied. The second layer or the figures was applied in natural color.

RELIEF MURALS

Basic Materials
1. Caulking compound or flour and salt.
2. Knife, spatula, cake icer.
3. Masonite or other sturdy background material.
4. Tempera or other types of paint.

Method for Making Relief Murals
1. A relief mural may be made on a masonite background or a material strong enough to support the weight of a caulking compound without cracking. Caulking compound may be purchased by the pound and mixed with water to the consistency of paint. It is then brushed, squeezed, or patted on masonite board. A knife or spatula will help in spreading the compound. A cake icer may be used to make thin lines. If a background of paint is to be used, it should be applied before the compound. The relief mural may be painted with various colors after the mural is completed.
2. A salt and flour relief mural may be made by mixing four parts salt with one part flour. Add enough water to make a consistency that can be squeezed through a paper cone or used with fingers. The map or other illustration is drawn on heavy cardboard and built up by adding the salt and flour mixture. Additional layers may be added when the first layers are dried. It may be painted when completed.

Care in Making Relief Murals
1. If using a caulking compound, study the directions for proper solvents to clean dishes and hands.
2. Mural should be suspended in a spot where it cannot be tapped or bent to prevent compound from peeling.

60

Teachers have found that it is highly desirable to have a workshop on sand casting before presenting it to children.

Plaster mixture is poured into a box of wet sand into which the design is depressed. Concrete may be used similarly.

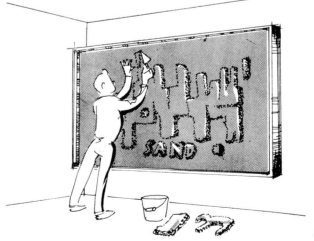

Sand cast objects in concrete or plaster cast objects can be used to develop an excellent mural. Consult a builder for methods of fixing the objects to a wall.

61

Telephone wire became Davy Crockett's bear, wire screen was used to make the fence, while copper wire made the longhorn steer. Other assorted materials were used to depict the life of this famous frontiersman.

MISCELLANEOUS MURALS

Basic Materials

1. Metal or plastic tubes, wire, screen, metal shavings, sheet metal, extruded and scrap metals; any type of glass; wood—any type of chips or mill ends or other pieces of wood; yarn, ribbon, string, cloth materials.

Methods

1. Many older pupils find it a challenge to create a structural mural with the endless varieties of materials available.

Care

1. Precautionary measures should be taken with some of these materials to prevent injuries and damage to children, equipment, and furniture.

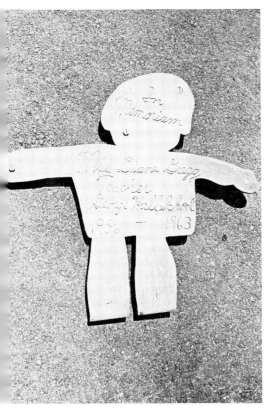

SAN MATEO SCHOOL MURALS

A mural program in the San Mateo Public Schools and shown on the next six pages demonstrates, in part, the scope of mural activities completed in one school district. Most of the murals were created under the direction of their Art Supervisor, Richard Sperisen. Photographs were taken by the San Mateo Public School System.

This eight-foot panel was made out of government surplus aluminum and brass by first grade children. Their drawings were transferred to the brass panel. Mr. Otis Master of the maintenance staff cut and mounted the panels for the children. One panel was dedicated to one of the teachers.

Quick drying exterior enamel was painted directly on canvas by first graders. The theme "Father of Our Country" was a part of a patriotic celebration observed by the entire school.

"What I would like to be"
is the title of this corridor
mural. It was painted on
canvas with tempera paint
mixed with a resin glue for
permanence.

The history of California
became more meaningful when
200 fourth grade children
participated in the creation of
this clay tile mural. Each six-
inch square tile was covered
with clay slip and glaze for
color.   After they were fired,
the tiles were adhered to the
redwood panel with special
glue which was prepared for
them by a local adhesive
engineering company.

Second graders painted a
series of pressed-wood panels
with nalcrete paint. These
panels are a part of a cafeteria
mural and panels are regularly
replaced by new ones as the
children create them.

64

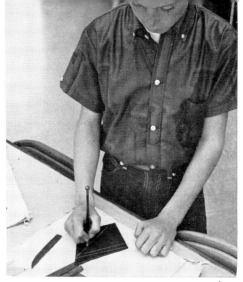

a.

b.

c.

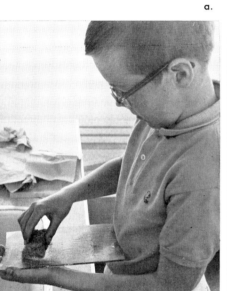
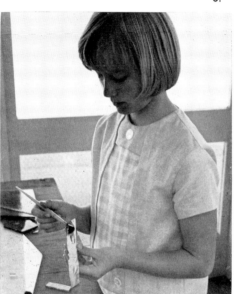

d.

e.

f.

a. Scrap colored glass was collected to make a stained glass window mural.

b. The glass was cut to appropriate sizes with a glass cutter. Safety measures were discussed, thus eliminating injuries.

c. After the pieces were cut they were then placed on a large table to correspond with the window to which they were later adhered.

d. Each piece had to be cleaned thoroughly. Instructions from a stained glass window artist were followed carefully.

e. The weatherproof adhesive was applied to each small piece which was then glued to the large window pane.

f. The final creation depicted the seasons of the year. It became a colorful addition to the school library.

a. and b. Objects of all kinds were impressed on six-inch square clay slabs to create floral designs. The tiles were then adhered with an epoxy to the 16-foot redwood obelisk.

c. The art clay was cut into six-inch squares. Floral designs were built up by either adding or by cutting away the clay base. Glaze was then added and the tiles were fired after which they were adhered to pressed-wood panels with durable glue.

d. One hundred and twenty kindergarten children pressed their hands into wet clay. This wet clay was then cut into six-inch squares which were fired and adhered to plywood panels.

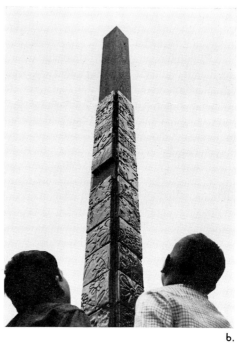

a.

b.

c.

d.

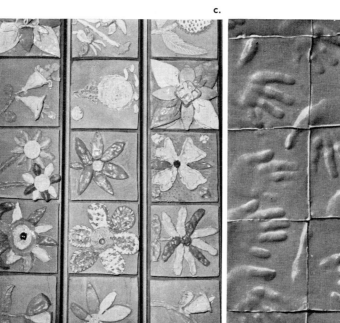

Mr. Benny Bufano, a well-known West Coast professional sculptor and muralist, helped these fifth and sixth graders create a mural.

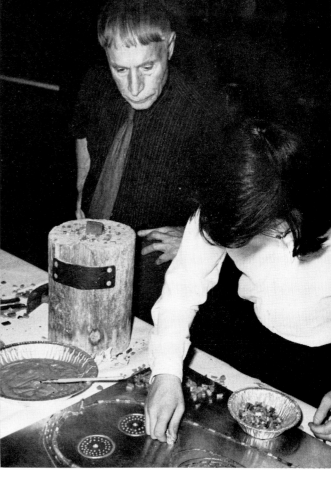

These children are grinding the tesserae in order to assure a good fit of each tile to the brass base.

Government surplus brass was carefully cleaned so that a specially-prepared adhesive would permanently adhere the tesserae to the brass.

The first verse of a poem written by the children describes their feelings:

Three years ago a man to Turnbull
(school) came.
Mr. Benny Bufano was his name.
He helped us dedicate a statue
With mosaics of every hue.

This is a portion of a 22-inch high and 75-foot long L-shaped mural on a wall of a school library. A wide variety of linoleum tiles were cut and glued to pressed-wood panels. About two hundred and forty seventh and eighth graders worked on this mural titled "Inspiration of America."

Educable mentally retarded children completed this ceramic, stone, copper, and glass mural for the entrance of their school. The rewards gained by working together from the first drawings to the completed mural were considered a very valuable sequence of experiences.

4

Care of Materials

A well-arranged environment appeals to most boys and girls. How the work space is to be used should be planned by the teacher, or teacher and pupils together. It is necessary that the classroom become a functional workshop with a place for everything and everything kept in its place. Thought and care must be given to the practical problem of where to store the working materials, tools, and equipment. Children prefer storage space that can be easily kept in order. Labeling the material and tool racks will help to keep an orderly room.

It is important that children have opportunities to develop initiative, cooperation, responsibility, and other desirable social traits by keeping the schoolroom neat and clean. If the teacher demonstrates interest in keeping an orderly room and also attempts to improve the room's physical conditions, children will reflect interest and a constructive attitude in their desire to help improve and care for the room.

Cooperative sharing of materials should be stressed. The day before the project is to start or as the project develops the teacher may find it desirable to set up standards through class discussion. Children may make suggestions and agree on their self-conduct, consideration of classmates, and cooperation with the group. Suggestions may be written on the chalkboard, some of which might be:

1. Walk slowly.
2. Talk quietly.
3. Take the amount of paint needed and return what is not used.
4. When painting, wipe excess from brushes on edge of can.
5. Paint accidentally dripped on floor should be quickly removed with a wet rag.

69

A palette is an inspiration to a young muralist. Milk-bottle caps glued to cardboard made this palette.

6. When painting is finished, immediately clean and put brushes away.
7. Place newspapers on floor while painting.
8. Keep paints handy while in use. Place on nearby table or desk covered with paper.
9. Wear apron or old shirts when painting to protect clothing.
10. Observe school safety rules.

Distributing and collecting should be so completely organized that this phase of art teaching operates automatically. Misunderstandings may be eliminated if the method employed is regular, orderly, and thoroughly understood and agreed upon by the teacher and children. The material in an art room belongs to the children; therefore, they must learn to care for it. Teaching children the feeling of responsibility will eliminate many of the problems of handling art materials. Some classrooms have found it expedient to have monitors whose responsibility it is to care for and distribute materials. Monitors may be rotated to develop social responsibility for all students.

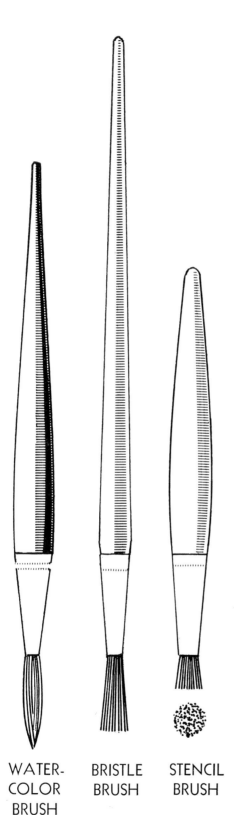

WATER-
COLOR
BRUSH

BRISTLE
BRUSH

STENCIL
BRUSH

PAINTBRUSHES

There are three brushes used most extensively in schools—the bristle brush, soft-hair brush, and stencil brush. The bristle brush can withstand more abuse than the soft-hair brush. If a brush is used in thick paint the bristle brush is recommended. The stencil brush is also a stiff bristle brush with a flat point. It is used for stenciling.

71

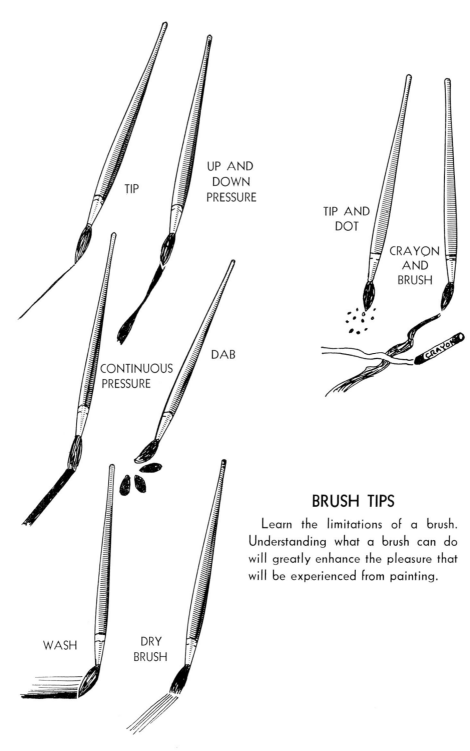

TIP

UP AND
DOWN
PRESSURE

TIP AND
DOT

CRAYON
AND
BRUSH

CONTINUOUS
PRESSURE

DAB

WASH

DRY
BRUSH

BRUSH TIPS

Learn the limitations of a brush. Understanding what a brush can do will greatly enhance the pleasure that will be experienced from painting.

STORING BRUSHES

A shoe box with holes properly spaced will serve as a temporary brush holder. Numbering both brush and hole assures the return of each brush to its proper place.

A 2- by 4-inch block of wood, drilled with holes large enough to support brushes, is a durable and convenient way of storing brushes.

Any can punched with holes will support brushes erect.

Vases for storing brushes have been the favorite of artists from the beginning of painting.

Mailing tubes are excellent storage units for a small number of brushes.

A spring from an old window blind attached to a block of wood is practical as a brush holder.

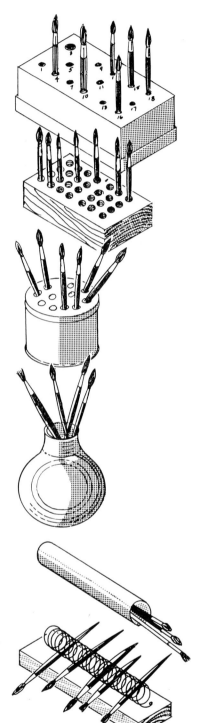

CARE OF A BRUSH

Do not abuse brush by forcing it against the paper.

The final washing of a brush should be done gently in the palm of the hand with soap and water. Do not permit the paint to dry into the ferrule of the brush.

Do not permit a brush to stand in a container of water for any length of time.

Avoid using the brush as a spoon or for mixing and dipping paint. Use a spoon or spatula.

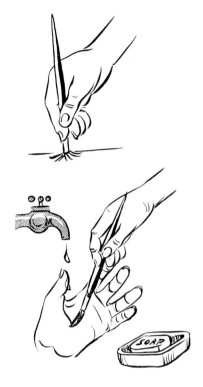

Teachers have found it helpful to organize materials in convenient locations which can be changed with new activities.

The following procedures are suggested for the care of brushes that have been used as indicated below:

Tempera, Calcimine, or Water Color

Wash with soap and rinse in plenty of water. Shape brush with finger tips to make the hairs perfectly straight and pointed. Place in a container with bristles up.

Shellac

Rinse in alcohol, wash immediately in soap and hot water. Shape and dry.

Oil Paint

Wipe on rags or paper toweling to get as much paint off as possible. Rinse in turpentine or solvent. Wash thoroughly in soap and water. Shape and dry. Keep bristles clean where they enter the ferrule. If this is not done the bristles will spread and the brush become shapeless.

Enamel and Lacquer

Follow the directions for cleaning your brush as recommended by the manufacturers of enamel or lacquer.

To Clean Brushes with Old Dried Paint

Tempera and calcimine will gradually soak out in lukewarm water if permitted to stand for a period of time.

Enamel and oil paint can be dissolved in any commercial paint remover. Wash remover out at once as it will dissolve the bristles. Then shape the brush with a thick soap mixture and allow to dry with the soap in it. This will force the bristles back into shape, although the brush will never be as good as if it were cleaned right after use. Before the brush is used again, soap should be washed out.

74

A large box with smaller boxes as separators and hand holes for carrying can serve as a tray in an art room. Several boxes the same shape can be conveniently stored one on top of the other.

Soft-drink containers are excellent units for handling and distributing jars of paint. If cans of the same size and shape are used, boxes can be stored on top of each other.

A simple Lazy Susan made of masonite, supported on a block of wood, serves as a revolving tray for easy access to paints.

Older students may enjoy making a simple tray for handling paints by soldering cans to a piece of tin. Similar trays can be made by gluing the cans to a piece of plywood with a non-water-soluble glue.

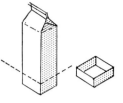

MILK CARTON

MILK-BOTTLE CAP

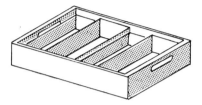

WOODEN BOX WITH PAPER DIVIDERS

CANNED-FOOD
CARTON

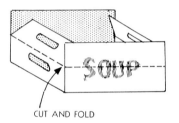

CUT AND FOLD

COMPLETED CARDBOARD
TOTE TRAY

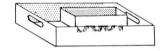

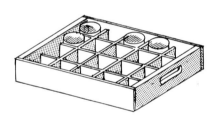

SOFT-DRINK CONTAINER WITH
BABY-FOOD CANS

MUFFIN TINS

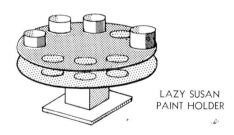

LAZY SUSAN
PAINT HOLDER

ART AIDS

For disposable paint pans, cut the bottom off a milk carton. Other waterproof paper containers will serve equally as well.

Metallic or paper milk-bottle caps, when pasted on a piece of paper, make a good paint palette. Other jar lids may also be used.

To reinforce the size of a cardboard food box, cut down the corners half-way and fold inward. This will become a practical tote tray.

Muffin tins of various sizes and types are always practical for paint trays.

BABY-FOOD CANS ON PLYWOOD

This paper cardboard carton tote tray becomes a convenient unit for distributing materials.

FOSTER ELEMENTARY SCHOOL, HOUSTON, TEXAS, BETTIE M. HAND, TEACHER

Newspapers spread over the floor will save a great deal of extra work at cleanup time.

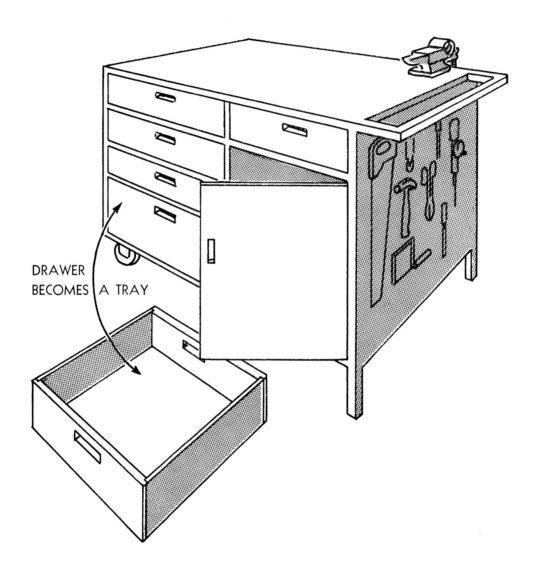

DRAWER
BECOMES A TRAY

Many art teachers are enjoying the convenience and mobility of a mobile art workbench. The one suggested here can be made in the school shops. The drawers are designed to be used as trays. Inexpensive plastic tote trays may take the place of handmade ones.

A classroom that undertakes large projects, such as making a mural, is usually confronted with the need of having quantities of material always available. Some-

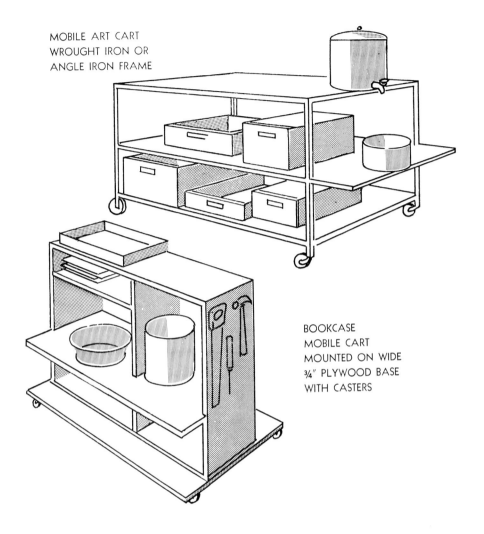

MOBILE ART CART
WROUGHT IRON OR
ANGLE IRON FRAME

BOOKCASE
MOBILE CART
MOUNTED ON WIDE
¾″ PLYWOOD BASE
WITH CASTERS

times it is necessary to paint the mural in the corridor or in a neighboring building. To solve this need, various types of mobile paint carts may be made or improvised. A grocery-store cart and basket may serve the need or a simple cart made of shelves on casters may be made in the school shop. Illustration No. 1 is a type that can be made of metal. Boxes of various types can be put on shelves to accommodate the materials needed while a water container with a spigot, available in most hardware stores, may be used for water. A large tin pan and pail may be combined to make a sink for dirty water.

Illustration No. 2 is a simple bookcase used for transporting art materials. The bookcase is resting on a large piece of ¾-inch plywood. The casters may be purchased from a hardware store.

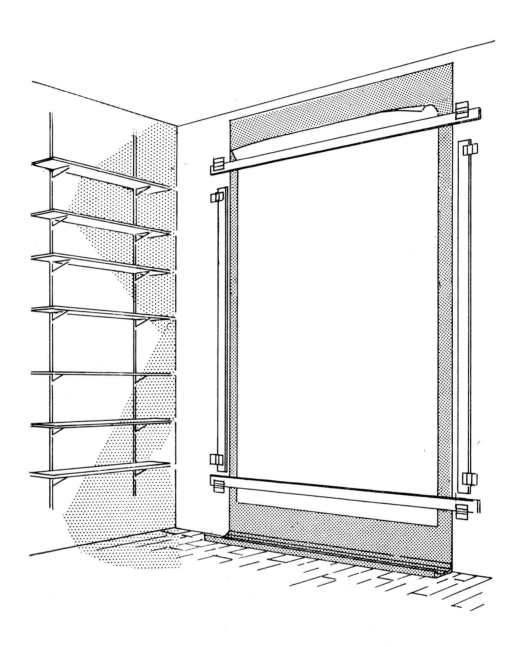

Some schools have installed a permanent linoleum background for mural painting. The linoleum is curled up at the bottom to catch the paint drops. Screen-door spring hinges are used to hold the paper on the wall while the children are painting.

5

Murals and the 3 R's

Most teachers seek ways of integrating art with other areas of learning. There is hardly an experience or a subject that does not lend itself to visual expression. Children also need the opportunity to reflect their experiences in some form. Art may provide this visualization. This creative procedure adds interest to the subject involved, provides a wider scope for freedom of expression, stimulates new art interests, allows art principles to be put into practice, and motivates children to actually bring to life subject matter which may otherwise be uninteresting and dull.

"Today, through such devices as project or enterprise, there is a strong tendency for art to flow from subject to subject until its identity as a separate subject field is often lost in the interest of the learning process.

"In the modern school, therefore, in order to enable the learner to profit more effectively from what is considered a more adequate learning situation, to allow him to express himself more significantly and to appreciate his surroundings more fully, and also to enable him to realize that cross-relations exist among all important human activities, the child is encouraged to select, as a basis of expression in art, his own experiences. Through art, the child of today gives form to the significant events in his life."[1]

Art can be incorporated into almost every phase of learning at both the elementary and secondary levels. Some teachers report that children learn and retain information much better if they can associate it with art. A classroom mural in history, for example, provides a natural integrative experience for children. While the school

1. Gaitskell, C. D. "Art and Crafts in Our Schools" published by Chas. A. Bennett Co., Inc., Peoria, Ill., 1949. Pg. 6.

81

SAN MATEO PUBLIC SCHOOL SYSTEM, SAN MATEO, CALIFORNIA, RICHARD SPERISEN, ART SUPERVISOR

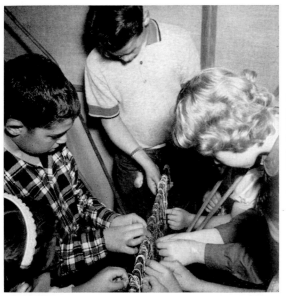

Creative art activities often lead to other unique projects. In this instance, surplus materials and handmade tiles were ingeniously combined to create a mosaic "bird in the round" in which a great many children participated. A number of learning processes and new skills were mastered.

art program does not always need to be correlated with other subject areas, the integrative process is a part of the school curriculum.

At the elementary level the core program helps both the child and teacher because in such a program a variety of experiences is related to a major theme or activity and there is frequently an opportunity for some phase of art. Most children can learn more about a week-end visit to the beach than they ever could from a teacher-described trip. The fantasies that a child may enthusiastically describe may not be labeled as a dramatic performance, but the freedom of expression with which the teacher encourages the child to tell his story may be excellent practice in play acting.

A teacher may select any one of many topics in any subject area for a mural project. It may be used as an incentive to seek additional information or learning, as a means of promoting interest in a specific study, as a culminating activity, as an opportunity to explore and experiment with various art materials, or a combination of all these. It is not always the one poem, story, play, or trip that is finally chosen to be illustrated in a mural or the completed mural that is important, but rather the satisfaction the children derive from creating the mural as well as exploring the material used.

As an example the author has selected the Thanksgiving theme to point out that even though an activity may appear relatively limited at first, it may be projected into virtually every subject area and activity in the school curriculum in innumerable ways. The ideas suggested here are but a few. The teacher and pupils will at all times want to use their own ideas in their own way.

THANKSGIVING MURAL

Objectives:

1. To understand how and why Pilgrims came to America and why Thanksgiving is celebrated.
2. To gain an understanding and appreciation of our American history and heritage.
3. To develop an appreciation of how we secure our food, shelter, clothing, and necessities of life in comparison with ways in which the colonists adapted their mode of living to their environment.
4. To understand the daily living conditions of the Pilgrims.
5. To understand how and why Thanksgiving has changed because of modern developments such as electricity, transportation, machinery, industrial specialization.
6. To afford an opportunity for children to explore, experiment, and experience new art media through a Thanksgiving mural which is integrated with a variety of subject areas.
7. To furnish an opportunity for children to plan, select, and organize materials.
8. To develop a thankful attitude toward the abundance, safety, and healthful

opportunities that our society provides today as compared to those of the Pilgrims.

9. To cooperate, carry out proposed plans, and evaluate an art activity.
10. To use a Thanksgiving mural to vitalize and correlate the learning processes in other subject areas.
11. To learn to work together.

Suggestions for the Mural:

A three-dimensional or constructed Thanksgiving mural may prove very interesting to children. Given the opportunity to express their ideas, children will develop others.

Children may explore the potentialities of materials they can bring from home, some of which may be: cardboard, charcoal, cork, rock, sand, thread, twigs, toothpicks, rubber bands, cotton, branches, colored yarn, sucker sticks. By encouraging children to study how these materials may become a part of the mural, the creative spirit will help them to utilize each item in a creative way. Through discussions they will discover how they can use certain items to make clouds, log cabins, fences, waves, trees, figures, animals, and any type of object.

Resources:

1. Informal class discussions of students' personal Thanksgiving experiences and plans for the ensuing Thanksgiving holidays.
2. Stories or poems found in the library or at home.
3. Committees to do research on early Thanksgiving, Pilgrims, and Indians.
4. Films, filmstrips, slides.
5. Play activities.
6. Attractive centers of interest that feature books, stories, or poems on Thanksgiving, flowers, pictures, fruit, or any items symbolic of Thanksgiving.
7. Scheduled television or radio presentation.
8. Assembly programs.
9. Recordings, tape recordings.
10. Pictures or post cards of a Thanksgiving theme.

Integration of Thanksgiving Mural with Other Subject Areas:

There are numerous stories, poems, and plays that may be read by the children to broaden their knowledge. Many valuable and unknown facts will develop an appreciation of the culture of the early American colonists and contribute vitally to children's learning.

In discussing the making of a Thanksgiving mural the class may wish to portray the first Thanksgiving as accurately as possible. Reading will be essential to determine such facts as the structure of the houses, relation with Indians, growing crops, transportation, means of preparing food, and any other pertinent facts in connection with the particular phase of the Thanksgiving mural to be made. This will also provide

Caulking compound on masonite produced this relief Thanksgiving mural.

children with the opportunity of learning where and how to locate material on a particular subject area.

Stories or poems may be created by the children and illustrated in the form of a mural. Certain ideas incorporated in the mural may provide excellent opportunity for choral reading. All the poems or stories written may not be used in connection with the mural, but they may be related in some other way.

Listening to music, singing songs, or expressing oneself through rhythmical activity contributes immeasurably to expressing oneself as well as learning to appreciate and understand good music.

Music may be studied by using a flannel-board mural. The rhythm of sounds may be easily "set to music" on the flannel board by the alert minds of children. Teachers may take or use this moment to set some sounds to music and later into a song to be played by the rhythm band or sung by the class. The discoveries in sound which the children make by themselves are vital and creative.

A Thanksgiving song may be learned or composed by the children on a flannel board. One student may arrange a staff on the flannel board with the key signature. Another student may place the time while other students may place the notes. The basic rhythm may be clapped out, perhaps punctuated by a tap-tap-tap with a stick on a drum thereby establishing a simple tonal pattern.

Young children may act out Thanksgiving rhythms such as planting seeds, cultivating crops, picking fruit, grains swaying in the breeze, animals walking.

Plays, skits, songs, or musical compositions may be written and later read or sometimes memorized to be presented as time and facilities permit. Pantomimes of Pilgrims, Indians, and Thanksgiving stories may be an enjoyable experience. A student can gain much by familiarizing himself with a character well enough to portray him.

In dramatization, there is a wide opportunity for the use of puppets. Children may make their own puppets, scenery, and sound effects featuring Indians, Pilgrims, the first Thanksgiving, and other Thanksgiving stories. The Thanksgiving mural on the wall is a most appropriate background for a play activity or Thanksgiving dramatization. Older students may develop this activity in more detail and present it to a younger group.

A Thanksgiving mural is almost naturally correlated with social studies. Many events of the Pilgrims and Thanksgiving which the children study in their social studies unit are incentives to make murals. Making a Thanksgiving mural will vitalize many important events such as historical developments, signing important documents, discovering new lands, culture of the past, and early modes of travel. Reading to gain knowledge of historical background to make the mural will prove more interesting than just reading a history or geography lesson.

Murals in connection with the Thanksgiving theme may indicate such arithmetical comparisons as the length of time it took early settlers to travel certain distances as compared with modern means of travel; rate of travel; population of northeastern states when pioneers first settled and present population; cost of first Thanksgiving dinner with one of today; and estimating and comparing living expenses then and now. In using a flannel-board mural, primary children may add and subtract the number of people, trees, or other objects in a Thanksgiving mural.

A study of health lends itself very well to a mural activity. There are limitless health topics or themes which may be used in connection with a Thanksgiving mural. A few are: foods, nutritional practices, physical care, then and now; a Thanksgiving menu that Pilgrims might have had and one of today; and other comparative health studies.

Science and its many related phases through a mural project will vividly show pupils the influence this subject has on the lives of people. Pupils may illustrate through a mural project how Indians and Pilgrims used stars at night to guide them, various signs of weather to plant crops, hunt, fish, and how trees, hills, stars, and forests were used to guide them in their travels. Through a mural they may indicate the various crops the early settlers and Indians grew; also, why some crops in the northeastern section of United States differ from those in other sections of the country.

Descriptive articles, short themes, or stories may be written about the scenes pictured in the mural. These may be posted on or near the mural or published in a school

Maps are often a form of murals. They may dramatize and illustrate graphically or three-dimensionally significant events in relation to specific locations and periods of time.

or local newspaper. With children who are just learning to read, words or sentences being studied may be appropriately pinned on a mural background or placed on a flannel board.

Evaluation:

The most important evaluation to be derived by the children is the basic satisfaction experienced during the learning process. A mural project serves its purpose if children grow in knowledge, develop an interest in things about them, learn to work and play together, and express themselves creatively.

Below are some of the specific points that a teacher might consider in determining the relative merits of the Thanksgiving mural activity.

1. Did the children gain a variety of experiences in related academic subjects?
2. Do they have a better understanding of the need for adequate food, clothing, shelter, health, safety, and recreational activities of early settlers?
3. Do they have a broader understanding of agricultural areas and what these people contribute in order to have a better world?
4. Do they have a better understanding of various services rendered through transportation, communication facilities, and modern scientific developments?

87

5. Do they have an increased understanding of nature, its effect upon our daily living and advances man has made in using nature to help them?
6. Do they have an improved understanding of our American heritage and the early history of our country?
7. Do they appreciate work of other peoples of the world?
8. Did they experiment with materials in a creative way in order to use each in its best possible way?
9. Do they have a better understanding of the need for every person to be an effective citizen in a community?

Culminating Activity:

It is important for children to highlight an activity with a culminating project, which may be an appropriate mural. Parents, friends, clubs, and other classrooms may be invited to visit and view the completed Thanksgiving mural. A program, dramatic play, or pageant carrying out the idea expressed in the mural, and using the mural as a stage setting, may be presented. It may be a puppet play from the English period of the day, or vegetable puppet play from a health activity. Choral readings, songs, games, dances, and short panel discussions may also be included, with every child participating in some way in the program. Costumes, scenery, room decorations, programs, and refreshments may be made by the children.

Movies may be prepared by the class. Oftentimes radio or television stations will cooperate in sponsoring interesting school ventures. The mural may be used merely as a school exhibit. Feature articles describing the Thanksgiving mural activity may be written for the school or local newspaper.

INTEGRATION OF MURAL ART WITH OTHER SUBJECT AREAS

Social Studies

One picture is worth a thousand words. By studying films, filmstrips, slides, post cards, pictures, books, and actual observation children learn about the homes, schools, cities, transportation methods, and other phases of life of our country as well as other peoples and countries. By using or studying about materials of other countries children better understand their arts, crafts and culture.

A mural can be used to show continuity or relationships in painting, drawing, or other art expression. A social studies mural by a second grade, "At the Farm," is an example.

At the Farm
Second Grade

Objectives:

To help children learn about animals found on a farm.

To help children become acquainted with farm products and their uses.

To show children importance of cooperation and responsibility through farm life.
To create a greater appreciation of farm and farm life.
To use a mural as a means of correlating the study of farms.

Resources:

Read, sang, and told stories about farm life.
Showed attractive pictures, films, and photographs illustrating farm life.
Visited a nearby farm.
Children cut out pictures from magazines pertaining to farm life and placed them on a bulletin board.

The Mural:

Children decided to make a mural using textured and various other materials.
Committees were formed to study and make animals, people, scenery, products, machinery, title for mural.
Mural consisted of a farm scene showing members of the family working, animals, machinery. Emphasis was on the pasting of textured materials. See below.

FOSTER ELEMENTARY SCHOOL, HOUSTON, TEXAS, MARY H. HEFNER, TEACHER

"At the Farm." Clouds were made of cotton; haystacks were made of sawdust pasted on the brown paper background; small sticks and yarn made the fence; textiles or fabrics made the clothing and curtains; title for mural was made of cutout paper.

Teacher's Evaluation:

Did the activity provide for free, informal association of pupils?

Did children have firsthand experience of some farm life activities?

Was it satisfying to children?

Were concrete and illustrative materials provided?

Were children given an opportunity to originate, plan, and direct activity through the mural?

Culminating Activity:

Parents and other classrooms were invited to see the mural.

Other subjects that might be used in a mural:

People Who Help in a Community	Holidays
Carpenter	Seasons
Milkman	Grocery Store
Postman	Bakery
Policeman	Library
Fireman	Clothing
Garbage Collector	Safety
Lawyer	How Animals Help Us
Doctor	How a Family Lives
Transportation	Homes for Everyone
Community Life	The Indian
World Neighbors	Pioneer Days

90

NUMBER STUDY

Number study murals may be made by line, bar, color, graph, figure relationships. Art contributes to number studies when children are permitted to work with various art materials and tools, to measure and determine weights and quantities, to use the right amounts of materials in formulas, and to determine the relationships of distances in drawings. Fractions may be explained on a mural by using different values of musical notes. For example, show the number of quarter notes it takes to make a whole, and other musical notes. Students may use arithmetic computations in drawing mural maps to scale and in studying the interpreting map keys. A flannel board may be used in teaching the meaning of the words parallel, vertical, horizontal, inch, foot, smaller, greater, shorter, longer, and other units of measure and weights.

In the actual making of a mural, arithmetic may be used in measuring the space for the mural, figuring the size of the mural and keeping items in relative proportion. Students may also use arithmetic in estimating materials needed for the mural project. When given an opportunity children will find suggestions for using numbers in murals.

Circus Mural
Primary Grades

Objectives:

To teach children a drill subject through participation in art.

To help children gain a knowledge of numbers through concrete and colorful objects.

To make number study come alive through art.

To stimulate interest in numbers through art.

To teach children by doing: actually placing the circus animals, people, and objects.

To teach children numbers by adding and taking away balloons, clowns, animals, and other objects on the circus murals.

To develop children's sensitivity to visual forms.

Resources:

Children listened to circus stories.

Pictures, slides, and films were shown on the circus and making of a mural.

With the help and permission of parents and principal, class attended the circus.

Children listened to circus music.

The Mural:

Children decided to make circus mural for a bulletin board with paper cutouts and painted scenes.

Committees were formed to do art work on circus scenes, animals, balloon men, clowns, colored balloons.

Children learned numbers by adding and subtracting animals, people and balloons on the mural, and items on the clown costumes. The study of the circus

A circus whets the interest of young and old.

gave additional number study by figuring costs of feeding various animals, costs of circus tickets, tabulating and numbering tickets for a circus show.

Teacher's Evaluation:

Were important parts of the circus included?

Did children learn number study through the circus mural?

Did everybody enjoy working on the mural?

Were colors descriptive of circus colors?

Did everybody cooperate and do his part?

Culminating Activity:

Games were played in the counting of balloons, animals, clowns, people.

Invitations were written to parents inviting them to come see the mural.

Mural was placed in the hall where other students could observe it.

Mural was also displayed as a unit on the circus at a local museum.

Local and school newspapers took pictures of the mural and published an article on it.

Other Subjects that Might Be Used in a Mural:

Farm Scene with Chickens and Eggs in Nests

Geometrical Shapes such as Circles, Rectangles, Triangles

Train with Cars

Baseball and Other Games

Flower Garden with Various Numbers and Kinds of Flowers

Parade with Animals, Clowns

Zoo Mural

Songs—"One Little, Two Little Indians"

Shopping in a Market

Pets

Adding Fruit to Trees

Making Change in Store

Birds

Barn Scene with Animals

Stories that Have Numbers such as "Three Little Pigs"

92

Products of various art activities are displayed to form an interesting circus project.

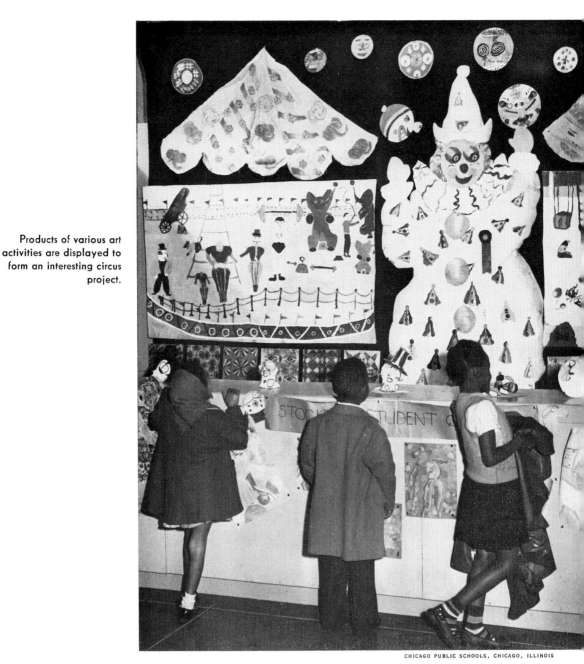

Children in special education classes also find mural activities a pleasant means of integration.

DRAMATICS

A backdrop or stage setting for a dramatic performance is a type of mural. An ordinary mural may also be used for other dramatic skits which do not require as much stage scenery.

Backdrop for Play, "Alice in Wonderland"
Sixth Grade

Objectives:

To provide an opportunity for everyone in the class to participate in some way in the creation of the dramatic presentation.

To help children develop an appreciation of stories.

To help children develop a relationship between art and reading.

To provide an opportunity for pupils to experiment with a combination of materials.

To build a mural backdrop for children's version of "Alice in Wonderland."

Resources:

Read story and showed films of "Alice in Wonderland," and on murals and tempera painting.

Visited museums, libraries, theaters to view and study large murals and stage settings.

Did research on how a backdrop for a stage should be made.

The Mural Backdrop:

Through class discussion the particular needs of the backdrop for the stage setting were decided upon.

Discussed the type of scene needed and how to achieve it.

Committees were formed to select size and texture of paper to suit needs of backdrop sketch scene, paint scene, put backdrop in proper place.

Sketches were drawn and enlarged to scale while backdrop was on floor.

Mural backdrop was painted with tempera paints after it had been properly hung.

Teacher's Evaluation:

Did the mural meet the objectives set up?

Did the mural develop a greater appreciation for stories?

Did it develop self-confidence, cooperation in working with others?

Did pupils gain ability to express observations from reading through art?

Culminating Activity:

Parents, classes, and organizations were invited to see the play. Description was given as to how the mural was made.

Article was written regarding the play and mural backdrop and put in local and school newspapers.

94

A stage backdrop can become an interesting "mural" activity.

Other Subjects that Might Be Used in a Mural:

Goldilocks and Three Bears	The Little Engine That Could
Three Little Pigs	Davy Crockett
Three Little Kittens	Peter Pan
Sleeping Beauty	Old Mother Goose
The Little Rabbit Who Wanted Red Wings	Who's Who in the Zoo
Hansel and Gretel	Nursery Rhymes
Little Black Sambo	Christmas Pageant
The Circus	Easter Play
The Brave Little Tailor	Spring Festival
Little Red Hen	Halloween Dramatizations

MUSICAL AND RHYTHMICAL ACTIVITIES

Musical and rhythmical activities may be integrated with almost any subject area.

Indians of the Southwest
Fourth Grade

Objectives:

To help children appreciate native beauty of Indian art in their clothes, homes, and ceremonies.

To help children become aware of the Indian influence in today's culture.

To develop racial tolerance.

To help children enjoy musical folklore.

To teach children how to make musical instruments for rhythmical activity and for display.

For children to learn to create their own Indian designs.

For children to learn through supplementary materials and mural activity how Indians progressed with our civilization's influence.

To help children learn through the making of the mural how Southwest Indians lived, worked, and played; to become familiar with some of their customs, ceremonies, weapons, homes, food, clothing, and ways of living today.

To help children learn group cooperation and to discover how each individual's efforts contribute to the whole mural.

To help children discover new ways in which art materials and discarded materials can be used.

Resources:

Most children are interested in learning about Indians. To extend this interest some children told of their experiences with Indians. Some parents volunteered to show movies and slides of Southwest Indian ceremonies taken on their travels.

Provided films, photographs, pictures, and stories regarding murals and Indians. Listened to records of actual Indian ceremonial music.

The Mural:

The class was divided into committees for making instruments, making the mural, developing rhythmical activities. Each child was identified with one group, but felt free to work with all groups.

Mural was painted with tempera paints by groups of children.

In addition to making the Indian background mural, children made Indian musical instruments, and created rhythmical activities.

Children enjoy re-enacting Indian ceremonial dances they have either seen personally or in an educational movie.

Teacher's Evaluation:

Did children become aware of Indians' rhythmical and musical activities?

Do the scenes depict the Indians' culture?

Were children creative in developing this activity?

Was the group cooperative?

Did children develop respect for other races?

Did children learn something of the value of time and how to organize work?

Were the objectives set up by the group fulfilled?

Culminating Activity:

Children put on a program. Songs were sung, instruments played, rhythmical activities given, poems recited. Mural background used.

Invitations were sent to parents inviting them to the program.

Presented program to other classes.

Other Subjects that Might Be Used in a Mural:

Listen to music and recreate it through art and rhythmical activities.

Music scale with children's interpretation.

Create a mural of favorite musical story, such as Peter and the Wolf, Grand Canyon Suite, or others.

Make a backdrop for a puppet minstrel show.

Depict a composer's life.

Create the history or evolution of various instruments.

Recreate dances through abstract symbols or designs.

Enact various classroom studies in rhythmical activities.

Attend or listen to an opera or concert and create a mural of what pupils saw or felt.

97

HEALTH

There are many phases of health study which can be made interesting and meaningful by being emphasized through a mural activity.

Mural on Posture
Third Grade

Objectives:

To show children what is good and poor posture.

To teach children the importance of good posture.

To help children become conscious of posture by relating it to a mural project.

To provide teaching as well as a learning experience through a posture mural.

Resources:

Films pertaining to health were shown.

Health posters, pamphlets, pictures, books were studied showing good posture.

School nurse was invited to discuss the importance of good posture.

The Mural:

Discussed children standing, sitting, walking correctly and incorrectly.

White butcher paper was tacked to the bulletin board.

Children stood against butcher paper while other children marked silhouettes.

Each child cut his silhouette, painted or colored clothes on the figure.

Paper figures were thumbtacked to the bulletin board.

Teacher's Evaluation:

Did the children improve their posture?

Did children enjoy making their paper cutout figures?

Did children learn the importance of good posture?

Culminating Activity:

Parents and other classrooms were invited to see children's paper figures.

Children played games guessing who the figures represented.

Made regular checkup on posture to see if it had improved.

Other Subjects that Might Be Used in a Mural:

Correct Way to Brush Teeth

Proper Amount of Rest

Proper Eating Habits

Right Kinds of Foods

Correct Play Habits

Nutrition—7 Basic Types of Foods

Food Required for 1 Day, 1 Meal

Care of Hair

Care of Hands

Care of Eyes

Importance of Body Cleanliness

Effect of Food on Body,
Posture, Skin, Bones, Teeth

WHEELOCK ELEMENTARY SCHOOL, LUBBOCK, TEXAS, MRS. ELEANOR BOWLING, TEACHER

How do we stand? By studying their own postures children become aware of its importance.

LANGUAGE ARTS

Finding, organizing, recording, and gathering pertinent information relative to a mural project is practical use of language activities. Learning to spell, looking up words in the dictionary, proper use of encyclopedia, developing and using card files are useful things to know and do. In a culminating activity such as a radio presentation, dramatization, or quiz program developing from a mural project, there is opportunity for creative growth in both oral and written expression.

Mural on Mexico
Sixth Grade

While this activity pertains to the Mexican border and was conducted to meet a local need, a similar procedure may be used in other sections of the United States in the study of other national groups and to fit particular situations.

Objectives:

To help children living in a border city to appreciate the local usage of Spanish.

To help children know and understand some of the colloquial usage of the Spanish language.

To develop a better understanding of other countries by learning to communicate efficiently whenever necessary.

To help children think freely and confidently in making a mural and learning another language.

To help children enjoy making a mural as well as gaining enjoyment and entertainment from having a knowledge of a neighboring country or another nationality.

Resources:

Visited the International Museum which deals with history of Mexico and its relations with United States; studied murals in the museum.

A border patrolman spoke to the class about his experiences with usage of the Spanish language.

Visited Santa Fe Bridge, El Paso, Texas, which divides Mexico from United States.

Encouraged students to watch Mexican television station to learn local Spanish language.

Encouraged children to listen to Mexican daily radio broadcasts.

Mexican newspapers, magazines, and other published materials were brought to class to view and study.

Viewed Mexican films to understand their culture.

Studied photographs of famous Mexican muralists.

100

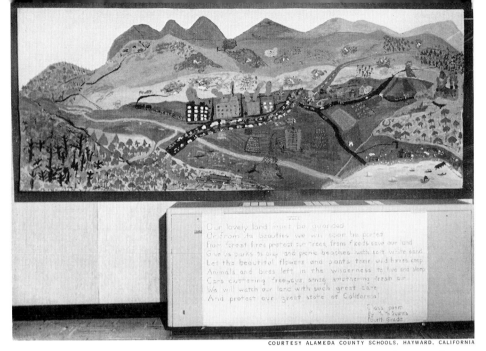

Poetry or any other language arts activity may be effectively highlighted by a mural.

The Mural:

Organized committees to secure information by reading, observing, listening to records, and visiting special Spanish class.

Each committee reported findings and made cutouts of words and sentences to be used on a flannel-board mural.

Searched for Aztec and Inca influences in fabric designs and other phases of Mexican life. Pictures or designs clipped from magazines, or drawn. They were then cut out, arranged on the flannel board and given Spanish and English names. Mexican artifacts throughout the room for decorative purposes and each given a Spanish and English title.

Teacher's Evaluation:

Were objectives set up by the class fulfilled?

Could pupils understand one another in their use of colloquial language?

Could pupils understand more of the Spanish language when a film was shown?

Culminating Activity:

Open house held with parents invited to view mural.

Viewed Mexican film to see if children understood any of the language.

Held a Mexican party, speaking the colloquial Spanish learned, and played Mexican games, with Mexican refreshments being served.

Invited Mexican children to school to present their dances, games, and songs.

Other Subjects that Might Be Used in a Mural:

Nature and Origin of Language	History of Printing
Famous Writers	Story of Alphabet
How to Read	Importance of Language Arts
Mural on Listening	Handwriting, Kinds and History
Oral Expression	Mural on a Class Newspaper

A tissue paper mural created by primary grade children of Baywood School, San Mateo, California.

Silk screen or prints may be used to make an effective mural.

Variations in paper mosaics can be successfully used at almost any educational level.

An egg carton Christmas tree assembled on a wooden frame is a pleasing arrangement of colors and shapes.

The three canvas paintings are framed with redwood. A series of pictures forms a type of panel mural.

The six-panel mural created by first grade children was painted on masonite using quick drying enamels.

Credit: Nicholas Roukes

Woods of all kinds cut into various shapes and symbols as well as selected objects were adhered to separate waterproof plywood panels which were assembled to form a mural twenty-four feet long. The panels were painted with acrylic paints. A large number of high school students participated in its creation.

On this pressed-wood pegboard panel acrylic paints were used to create a delightfully colorful symphony of symbolic musical instruments for the Conservatory of Music in San Francisco.

Credit: Lucienne B. Dimitroff

Credit: Nicholas Roukes

Acrylic paints are very resistant to all kinds of weather conditions. Mr. Nicholas Roukes (left), Senor Jose Gutierrez (center), and a French artist Claude Blin (right) are painting a mural in a swimming pool in Cuernavaca, Mexico.

Juan O'Gorman, the designer of the famous library mural at the Nationale University of Mexico City, stands in front of the entrance to his home. This multi-colored mural is created with local volcanic stones.

Credit: Nicholas Roukes

104